I0079070

MEN OF

THE JUNGLE

ION IDRIESS

ETT IMPRINT
Exile Bay

This 20th edition published by ETT Imprint, Exile Bay 2021

This book is copyright. Apart from any fair dealing for the purposes of private study, research, criticism or review, as permitted under the Copyright Act, no part may be reproduced by any process without written permission. Inquiries should be addressed to the publishers:

ETT IMPRINT
PO Box R1906
Royal Exchange NSW 1225 Australia

First published by Angus & Robertson Publishers 1932.
Reprinted 1932 (two), 1933 (two), 1934, 1936, 1937, 1938, 1939, 1941, 1942, 1943, 1947, 1948, 1949, 1951, 1953, 1955.

First electronic edition published by ETT Imprint in 2021

Copyright © Idriess Enterprises Pty Ltd, 2021

ISBN   978-1-922473-44-8   (pbk)
ISBN   978-1-922473-45-5   (ebk)

"Most of the illustrations are from photographs kindly lent by Mr Cecil Le Souef. They originally appeared in his father's great work Wild Life in Australia." I.L.I.

Cover: *Gossip Among the Mia-Mias,* photograph by William Le Souef.
Cover design by Tom Thompson

CONTENTS

FOREWORD

IT is a pleasure to write this brief Foreword to *Men of the Jungle*. Mr Idriess's vivid pages recall busy days when Cooktown was lively with prospectors from northern Peninsula goldfields: when men from the south-western tin-fields, from the beautiful Bloomfield and those wild outposts, the Scrub Camp and China Camp, made the old town merry.

These men came from fields the tracks to which were blazed by such path-finders as the brothers Baird, Christy Palmerston (that super-scrubman), John Dickie, of Peninsula fame, and other wonderful bushmen.

I remember well Idriess and his mates, Norman and Charlie Baird, and the gold they found on the Daintree track. Dick Welch, the Pierce brothers, the settlement at the Bloomfield, and the boys of the Scrub and China camps, too, are all known to me; and I am pleased to meet them again in *Men of the Jungle*. The book gives fine and true pictures of the lives led by our boys up here.

They are grand boys; and it's a grand country – this North of ours.

CHARLES PATCHING
"The Father of Cooktown"

PREFACE

THE publishers have asked me to write an account of the more adventurous part of my life. *Men of the Jungle* is a first instalment. At the time, the experiences here told did not appear to me very adventurous – nor do they now. But city folk, I find, look at these events differently to those familiar with the vicissitudes of a wanderer's life. It is for my readers to judge. If they show-by the only test publishers accept-that they like this book, another will follow, giving the story of my wanderings in other fields with other mates.

How Norman and Charlie will smile when they read these chapters! They are still in their beloved home district, the Bloomfield. But the last I heard of Assan, venturesome son of a Malay pirate, was that he had sailed away in his tiny cutter on vengeance bent, seeking a certain Filipino, last heard of in the Aru Islands, off the coast of Dutch New Guinea. Old Antonio and Philip Johnson, swarthy sea-rovers, have sailed on their last voyage, followed to the Shadow Land by kindly George Stewart, the old hatter of Mount Molloy. Old Tommy the Chinaman has gone there too.

The Pierce brothers are still at the Landing, and Frank Crowley, I believe, is still at Mount Mollov. Some of the Olufson family are at the old home on the Upper River, but I last saw the father and mother in Cairns. Nearly all the others mentioned are "going strong," although there has been a scatter amongst the coloured folk at the settlement. Many of my old aboriginal friends, I am sorry, or glad, to say (I am not sure which), have gone to their Happy Hunting-grounds.

One word about the Nature notes the reader will find here and there through the volume. It will be obvious that I am no scientist. I have written only of what interested me in that fascinating tropical world.

For the rest, if the reader learns from this book something of the natural wealth, the variety, the beauty, of one small spot in this wonderful land of ours, I shall be truly pleased.

Most of the illustrations are from photographs kindly lent by Mr Cecil Le Souef. They originally appeared in his father's great work *Wild Life in Australia*.

Ion Idriess

Wyalla Plain Aboriginals, early 1920s.

I

THE JUNGLE CAMP

GLOOM and stillness, yet teeming life. A million trees, a million vines under a canopy of leaves, blocking every ray of sunlight. The air cool and sweet, it looked almost "blue" so riotously green was the vegetation. Very peaceful, seemingly, is that primeval northern Queensland jungle-scrub.

A hoarse coughing grunt sent me flying behind a tree. I'd left even the revolver away back in camp. Ass! As I peered with beating heart, the rattling of lawyer-canes, the swishing of palm-fronds, then the squelching of his big splay hooves told that he was coming down there in the moss-covered ravine.

Yes! a gleam of tusks curving from a long snout and the massive chest and shoulders of "Rungooma" the man-killer came into view. He was rooting amongst the moss for the bloated four-feet-long, phosphorus-coloured worms, like flabby snakes in blue and green and purple. A spray of vines caressed his ears and little, wicked eyes. Broad leaves draped his lean, mud-caked flanks. His snout appeared gingery, his body a dirty black Secure in that he had neither seen nor smelt me, I noted a slim tree nearby, then gazed fascinated at this wild boar that had killed two men. If that grizzly old swine charged, he'd need to be greased lightning to catch me.

This notorious boar was discussed wherever native campfires glowed; his deeds were "sung" in corroboree , told in breathless story. Many an ambitious warrior would have loved to "get" Rungooma, had he only dared try. Eagerly I spied on this brute of the jungle. The things of the Wild always interested me in those years of roaming. Perhaps because in the primeval bush the animals and birds and fishes enter so closely into a man's everyday life that he gets to know them almost as he does his horse.

Rungooma scented a worm. His powerful shoulders pushed his head into the loam and the leathery snout ripped it up like a ploughshare. The tit-bit disappeared to an ecstatic gurgling.

Those monstrous worms are weird things; they belong rather to the world of diprotodons than to present days. The jungle is their home, particularly *where* the foliage for months of the year is adrip with rain, and the thick carpet of decaying leaves becomes alive with minute phosphorescent insects. These cling to the worms as they crawl along. On exceptionally moist days the big crawlers fairly glow as if alight inside. Some really *are* "alight;" there is living phosphorus in their skin. They progress much as a caterpillar does. The worm stretches out till it looks like a long strand of elastic, then the head-end grips the earth and holds while the rest draws up to it in ever fattening sections, like greasy green rubber. It then repeats the performance. Occasionally the belly of a black snake shows a phosphorescent glow, but you can only see it as he slides up and over a hanging root.

Rungooma pushed off down the ravine, deep-chested grunts expressing his content. He was boss of the world when armed man was not about. As he pushed through the vines they slid up over his snout and back and clattered away behind. Seen side on, his big curved tusks gave an ugly curl to his lip. He left tracks in the moss like those of a bullock.

I hurried back to camp, eager to tell my mates that I had actually seen Rungooma. Oh for a rifle to have shot him and so felt the triumph of a native warrior at a big kill! Man is a bloodthirsty brute, especially when he is young.

It was a happy camp, that jungle home of ours. A hard camp mind you, and a hard life. But then we were strong as colts and full of life. Even to swear was a pleasure. If it had been an easy life, with nothing to fight against, we would not have been nearly so happy.

We were camped right in the centre of the Divide, on top of the world in the heart of the jungle. The streams on one side of the watershed fell in hurrying cascades into the soughing gorge of the Daintree , those on the other fell into the· sunlit forests of the Bloomfield. Often on misty mornings we breathed the very clouds. We have watched a cloud float upon a mountain summit and roll upon its cap of treetops. Billowy mists would break off and glide down the mountain sides to curl in floating wreaths of lace vainly seeking to penetrate the foliage.

Exactly at our camp was the crossing-place of the native route over the mountains separating the Daintree from the Bloomfield. There was no pad, although we called it "the native pad;" it was just the only accessible way through the jungle. Very occasionally a file of natives would silently appear, visitors or messengers travelling to some tribe away down below.

There were three of us, Norman, Charlie, and I. They called me Jack: it was absurd to be called Ion out there. Every man should pick his name to suit his environment. Norman and Charlie had a touch of coloured blood; their father was the famous pioneer Robert Baird who had opened up China Camp when he and Christy Palmerston brought the first cattle overland. He had given the boys a good education. Norman was a handsome chap, tall, straight, and slim, with clean-cut features, a nice smile, and the brownest of brown eyes. Quiet and dreaming in temperament. Charlie was shorter and nuggety, with thick, jet-black eyebrows, a determined chin, exceptional shoulder muscles, and simply tireless legs. He was a fearless chap, very quick to help a mate when in trouble, but inclined to be moody at times. Charlie was a bundle of energy when anything was doing, and a grimly determined devil when aroused; I've seen his black eyes blazing with fury.

Both were born bushmen, with that rare trait of being at home in the scrub as well as in the forest. Their life was lived in two worlds, the white and the black. They were as familiar with the campfires of the natives as with the homes of the whites. The deep inner life of the natives, the "secret life" to which but very few white men have ever been admitted, was theirs as freely as was the totally different outlook of the whites. Their father and big Bill Baird (speared by the blacks, finder of Mount Romeo and the Batavia River gold) and such noted bushmen as Palmerston, Hislop, and Stucke, had taught the lads everything from the white man's point of view.

On the other hand, as children they had learned the story of life within the gunyahs of the blacks, and, later, around the council fires. So the boys knew intimately the black and the white, the hopes and fears, the fights and feuds and bitter vengeances, the so different outlook on life, of the two races.

Our camp was simple: necessarily so, for we had to carry it on our backs some miles from China Camp, then up three thousand feet of precipitous mountain before entering the jungle. A small tent, billycans and tools, several fifties of flour, tea and sugar, a rifle, matches, and prospecting-tools comprised our outfit. Scrambling up that mountain with a sixty-pound weight on one's back was no joke; but we did it with a laugh even while we sweated. To make the provisions hang out we used to live on the rifle, on bushcraft, and luck.

I hear that camp now, in my dreams. In softest tones with notes of liquid silver it calls, and calls again: the velvet night gemmed with fireflies; somewhere a hammer-bird tap, tap, tapping; the tree-scented air; the whispering silence. Charlie sleepily murmurs:

"The creek is singing real sweet to-night."

The tent stood in a tiny clearing on a corner bank, walled around by trees except on the Big Creek side where the water flowed over moss-covered boulders, walled in by terraced banks. A baby creek fell spilling into it, in singing cascades that tinkled past the tent door. This was our "Singing Creek." A thousand arms of the jungle stretched eager fronds across it to coil around palm and fern.

We slept in of mornings until hunger awoke us, for those branches and leaves overhead blocked all sunlight until we had felled trees and made the little clearing open to blue sky. The afternoons were short for the same reason, the sun was "down" in the scrub though he still blazed brightly in the open forest miles away.

The jungle was silently but mercilessly antagonistic to us, always seeking to smother us. Where we felled a tree or cleared the ground in dire necessity, immediately right there the jungle sent up eager shoots to cover the bareness. Greedily it encroached on our clearing from all sides; tendrils would come in the night creeping towards us from the trees; yellow tips of plants arose in our very galley. Along every track we cut, the jungle almost at once stretched out branches and vines to close the gap. It would have grown things out of our bodies had we only slept long enough.

"It is ceaselessly fighting," said Norman one day, "not only the jungle but everything in it, fighting to live. See, there is a fight now!"

He pointed into the crystal-clear creek where a greenish-yellow water-snake chased by a vicious grey eel had sped under the bank to wedge himself behind a trellis of roots. The reptiles slipped in and out amongst the roots, savagely biting as opportunity occurred. The snake dodged with uncanny swiftness every rush of the eel who snapped in fury with a mouth hideously armed with needle-pointed teeth. Once the snake broke away and sped for the open creek but the eel was on him in a flash biting, plunging, snapping. The snake doubled back and reached the sheltering roots with the eel at his tail. Surely, and with almost reasoning tactics the eel wedged him farther in despite his frantic twistings, and as he made his last desperate dive outwards, bit him clean in halves.

"Everything does that," said Norman softly. "Everything is eating something else; there are cannibal things in the jungle, flowers that eat living things, and insects that eat their own lovers. Here, men sometimes eat one another too. If ever you see them never let on you know, or you, too, will go on the cooking-stones."

We had a visitor at times. Though we swore at him on occasion, he treated us with disdain. Coming home for dinner one day we espied him using as a bridge a bean-tree we had felled across the creek. He was a cat with a long, pointed nose disdainfully sniffing to a twitching of white whiskers. Daintily queer, he stepped solemnly along, his long, thin body arched like a boomerang, his bushy tail laid back along his spine and poked out over his head like the bowsprit of a boat. His coat was a silver-grey starred with spots like new threepenny bits. His cold, staring, watery-blue eyes had never a wink in them.

He would possess our camp in stately fashion and nose around for scraps. A hopeless hunt-we were always too hungry. When we had shot a pig or a turkey, however, he would commandeer a feast of bones. He didn't call regularly, any old time seemed to suit him; and we had to keep perfectly quiet or he wouldn't come at all. His attitude towards us was always one of cold disdain. Perhaps he believed himself to be unique.

This queer cat of ours didn't mew; but the catbird did. That lively customer used to hop up and down on the long-stalked plants on the terrace edge opposite. He gave us cheek at breakfast-time; most pointedly he insisted that we take notice of him. He loved acrobatics and would swing on a fruit-bearing creeper that hung from an elm-branch and rock himself to and fro mewing like a smooging cat. And cat I believed it to be until the morning I noticed Norman wink at Charlie .. He was an astonishing mimic that bird; he would chuckle like the turkeys, hiss like a snake, scold and chirrup in imitation of other birds. This feathered comedian in green and gold studied us craftily. One day I glanced around at the sound of someone washing a dish in the creek. I listened in surprise, for Norm and Charlie were both in camp, smoking by the galley. There it came again, that rasping swirl of gravel on tin as a man washed a dish of dirt. It took me some time to realize that the feathered rogue opposite was really imitating a gold washer. As time went on he improved his repertoire by imitating the stirring of a spoon in a pannikin, the striking of a match, the rasp of the file as we sharpened the axe. He had a language of his own *too,* queerly harsh notes followed by clear liquid ones, low and sweet, that rang *out* brimming with happiness.

The terrace flats were the hunting-grounds of birds, lively water-rats, comical squirrel things, and other jungle life, seeking the yams and roots, bulbs and berries and fruits that grew there.

In whichever direction we sought to walk from the camp, unless stealthily on the war-path after something to eat, we had to swing the broad-bladed cane-knife and cut our way. The lawyer-vines were a special pest. In places they covered acres: their faggot-like butts with curving palm-like leaves grew many lengths of coiling, twisting cane, often a hundred feet long-nature's wire entanglements. Cruel hooked barbs' on these long strong stems were the "Come-back-quicks." As we brushed past they would rip into our flesh and drag us back with a gasp. Not content with running along the ground, these canes would often climb the tallest trees to seek sunlight, and run out over the treetops. Often, from there, they hung down in ropes, overhead traps for the unwary. The canes that coiled on the ground, though, were a very real menace when a man was pig-hunting, tripping him up should he be forced to run. That was how Rungooma had gained his two victories.

Our camp was south of Cooktown, and the nearest storekeeper was close on a hundred miles away. Every scrap of civilized food we ate we had to carry for miles on our backs. We were always hungry. We were working hard, but hunting for food was the hardest work of all. Still, that had its compensation in the thrills of attainment. And what a lot one learned of the scrub and its inhabitants! We got to know almost the life-histories of animal and bird, fish and shrub. We had to learn what the first two ate, in order to catch and eat them; we had to find where yams grew thickest before successfully seeking the yam-eaters, and which trees grew the berries the pigeons ate. We had to scout the ravines for wild pig and learn where and when the scrub turkeys fed. We had even to learn the play and love-making of the Wild-all to keep the larder supplied. As the years went by, my mates and I grew very close to the heart of the Wild. On hushed days and nights I could almost sense the great heart beating.

Some few men merge right into the heart itself. They are perhaps "queer" and are very few and far between. I have met one or two in the Far North, men who have slipped right back until they have become literally Children of Nature. They can do that phenomenally hard thing, exist in the bush on what their cunning, endurance, and sharpened "animal" intelligence secure them. They have earnestly assured me that animals and birds "talk," that even fishes, by varying twists of the tail, cause vibrations which carry distinct meanings, that flowers send messages by scent.

These men I write of can imitate and bring to them almost every animal and bird in the bush. Two in particular could even smell animals quite a distance away. They lived (are living now for all I know) an extraordinarily lonely life. They could tell the meaning of the least sound, hearing sounds that often I could not. Even the sigh of the trees carried a distinct message for them of wind or rain, of coolness or heat on the morrow. They have assured me that trees have a joy in living and can feel and understand.

Flowers, they say, are quite live things, realizing the purpose of their colouring, regulating by a law of instinctive feeling their perfume, and controlling the beauty or guile which has been given them to attract insects and birds.

These men taught me so many secrets of the jungle that at last I came dimly to realize what a vast secret the jungle really is.

2

THE THIEF

GOLD took us to the mountains, and gold held us there until Nature starved us away. It was a ruthless fight. But gold lured us back again and again.

That was excellent quality gold, heavy little pieces that rattled in the dish and shone up with a provoking yellow that stirred our senses. There is something in a speck of gold that can set a man's heart on fire. Every fair-sized speck I got gleamed up at me as if it possessed something above its material value. I have met men who believe that gold lives and grows. As Norman and Charlie examined their pieces, they, *too,* felt the influence-fairly loved them as it were. But those specks were hard to find, there was a lot of Queensland mixed with them. "Nature hides her secrets well."

Gold puts the acid test on men and soon proves whether they are trusty mates or not. Good men have lost their souls after striking the yellow tempter. Don't gloat over gold, as men feel impelled to do in the quiet camp at night. The more a man handles the stuff the stronger the lust of it grows upon him, Those dull yellow lumps exert a sinister influence; they *claim* a man. Each has its own striking shape, its colour, its feel, its hold on his memory. He licks a piece to see it shine and it leaves its touch on his tongue; he weighs it broodingly yet again and it leaves its weight in his hand. Later he dreams of the stuff, hidden cunningly away under the fire-place. By day, it occupies his mind consciously and subconsciously as he works. Yes, it is dangerous to gloat over gold lest it become a devil terrible to fight against.

I felt strangely pleased when on a distant trip from the camp Norman pointed across a sea of mountains and told me I was the first white man to penetrate that jungle. He should know, for his Dad and Palmerston were the first white men in the district, while the boys were born in China Camp, the little tin-mining camp down there in the forest valley towards the Roaring Meg. When children, their Dad had taken them into the jungle edge in search of gold, and they had won a little too. That had been a hurried trip: trouble broke out amongst the Chinese gangs down below, and the Dad had to return. Now the boys and I were carrying on where the old pioneer left off.

Men had prospected the open forest country around China Camp, and penetrated up into the scrub towards the seaward side of the mountains. Only Baird had ventured on our jungle side.

It is easy to understand why. In the open forest you can see the ground, the creek and ravine bottoms, the outcrops of rock on the spurs, the hills near and far away. The country is easy to prospect. More than that, you can go anywhere with horses, for any length of time, while overall is the sunlight illuminating the book of Nature spread before you.

But in the jungle all you see is the gloom, and trees hemming you in, and roots underfoot. Over much of the country you cannot even walk unless *you* cut your way. The jungle not only buries her secrets under the earth, she smothers the earth under green stuff as well.

One morning we were whistling along to work when Norman sprang back as a branch silently dropped to thump at his feet. He looked around with a smile, saying evenly:

"A close go!"

That evening, around the galley fire, we discussed how a man develops jungle-sense in various respects -in danger for instance. Norman in one case, walking out to the galley one black night suddenly stood still, his bare foot poised above a snake. The same thing has happened to me, and Charlie had a similar experience with a death adder. During one of our walkabouts, Charlie, out in the lead, suddenly stood perfectly still, staring into a screen of leaves. One step more and he would have plunged straight through and down over a dizzy precipice. And there was the night when Norman couldn't sleep. Again and again he got up and went out into the clearing. Next morning at breakfast he said with a nod: "That big hickory over there isn't safe."

"Looks solid enough," said Charlie after a pause.

"It will fall-I feel it."

That evening, coming home from work, Norman, in the lead, walked very slowly when coming near the Big Creek. He stood quite still on the bank, and we stood beside him, staring across at our camp in the clearing. In the stillness of a windless day the topmost leaves of the big hickory trembled, its higher branches gently moved; without a sound its crest leaned slowly over as it came with gathering momentum. A moment later and with a thunderous crash it flattened the galley in a wreckage of splintered branches.

Several times this queerly imperative "Hold back!" has held me with my face but an inch from a stinging-tree leaf. That may not sound awful, but it is. A proper sting from that broad-leafed shrub means agony for many hours; the sting itself is felt for days, often weeks afterwards; a twitch is felt months afterwards if you touch the part with water. Men have gone raving when badly stung; a horse will gallop frantically and probably dash himself against a tree. Strangely enough, cattle occasionally eat the stuff. Does this fact mean that its juices have some antitoxic value, on the principle of one poison killing another? Any dog that touches the leaves, suffers agony, whimpering and shivering like a man with acute malaria, all drawn up with its tail between its legs, and every hair on end.

The stinging-tree leaf is a pleasing bright green, and occasionally as broad as a plate. The undersides of the leaves are covered with microscopic white spikes, resembling minute crystals. These apparently cause the sting. The leaves when dried up and long dead on the ground, still retain their virulence.

There is no known cure for the agony. Some men say the juice of the tree itself provides one. The best thing to do is to quickly scrape down the arm with the blade of a knife. This possibly removes invisible prickles before their poison properly enters the system. When it does, lumps rise up under the arms and in the groin. Men burn the hair off their arms and legs when stung, hoping to burn out the prickles, or seek relief in other more or less mad ways. I, myself, stood on my head against a tree, among other things.

When cutting a track, a man is always wary lest the cane-knife brings down a stinging-leaf from the foliage above. If a tree is disturbed by the jerking of the vines it sheds a something, a powder maybe, that sets one sneezing and running at the nose and eyes. There are different species of stinging-tree; some are large trees; but the big, broad-leafed shrub is the terror.

There is too an "electric" vine in the jungle, a tough creeper with a raspy feel. Grasp it the right way and you receive a faint shock very suggestive of electricity.

There is also a quaint little "electric" caterpillar in those scrubs that is practically invisible on the leaves. It is extraordinarily broad for its inch length, and has a yellow coat decorated with a line of purple spots. Its flattish body is arrayed with stiff spikes. When one's hand touches this thing one feels a nasty little tingling jar that reminds him of a battery. No bird, I believe, eats it. It has no legs; its underpart resembles sticky rubber with which it gets a grip on the leaf and pulls itself along. It only comes to light during the rainy season, and then it only travels on the undersides of the leaves.

One day as we talked of those scrubs yet awaiting the white man's foot, a shadow passed across the creek and vanished in the foliage. Our trained eyes spotted him on a branch directly above the tent, his head, like a scarlet flower, peering down from among the leaves. Charlie reached for the ever handy rifle. "Crack!" and a black body struck branch after branch to thump down at our feet.

What delight it was to shoot a scrub turkey! It made such a splendid meal. We depended for almost all our meat on the rifle. Luckily, the turkey is inquisitive, the smoke from the galley fire as it curled up amongst the trees induced them to investigate. I rather believe they smelt the smoke when they could not see it. The white tent intrigued them, too, as did the men smoking or moving about. So, sometimes a tasty dinner brought itself obligingly to the camp, the body at times flopping right on the tent if we were quick and straight with the rifle. As a rule, the big black-plumaged bird scouted our camp on foot. Norman's trained ears would hear a stealthy rustling amongst the undergrowth. Still as death, with cocked rifle, we would wait, to hear presently a hesitant clucking, then a stealthy rustling. He would either vanish or we would spot his purplish-white wattles and neck craning from the jungle edge that circled our little clearing – and that would be the end of him.

We liked turkey shooting. It did not mean needless killing, but a fat bird for the pot to be enjoyed by three hungry men. Like the turkeys, we lived to eat to live. These birds delighted in the terraces lining the creek-flat banks that, were a maze of lawyer-palms, broad-leafed water plants, cycads, ferns, and shrub. Here they scratched and clucked while digging for the succulent red bulbs of the ginger plant. Among the tall tree-trunks at any terrace edge one might listen, until the silence closed in till one felt one's body was a thousand ears. Then, quite distinctly would come a clucking and scratching deep within the undergrowth. Like an eager python one would crawl through a wilderness of plant-life towards the sound. If one solitary lawyer-cane cracked back upon its mates, then only silence, scratched arms, and disappointment awaited one at journey's end.

We roamed the mountain sides seeking turkeys' nests. So, to our disgust, did the wild pigs; they gobble turkeys' eggs with delight. The big birds were far more often located on the ground than among the branches. With outstretched neck and swaying tail they would run swiftly through the undergrowth – and be gone. But startle one, and he would cluck agitatedly and dart off, rise heavily, flop up on to the nearest branch, and peer from that vantage for the danger below. The hunter had to shoot quickly, for the lively bird would hop from limb to limb ever rising to disappear in the foliage overhead. We always used a rifle: a shot-gun would have been useless had we met a pig.

Memory recalls one big nest, because of corresponding disappointment. Standing beside a kauri-gum that towered in lonely beauty, I listened. From a distant height the deep-toned call of a wompoo pigeon broke the silence that harmonized so with the cool gloom. Then, quite a distance away down the mountain slope, sounded a distinct scratching. A man would never hear so small a sound so far did he not "go into the silence" first. On quick noiseless feet over those roots and loam and decayed vegetation I stalked down through the avenues, then slowed up and listened. Yes, quite close now, busy scratchings and flurry of showering leaves! Turkeys renovating their nest! Less cautious because they would be so busy, I pressed downward and peered over the flange of a giant fig-tree. There was the mound of twigs, earth, and leaves, six feet high with a tremendous base. The labour of generations of turkeys must have gone to the building of that nest. Two birds were busy now; the eye first caught the reddish head, purplish-white wattles and neck, the larger, blacker body of the male. Both had their heads down and backs towards me. Scratching first with one foot then the other they sent behind them a continuous shower of leaves, unerringly flicking them clear of the undergrowth. The male clucked at his labour, comically reminiscent of the grunting of a hard-working man. The brownish hen was putting her weight into it but with a condescending air, as if she fully realized it is the male bird's job to keep the home in repair. Other birds had long since scratched the earth bare for a surprising distance from the mound, so that these builders had to go right into the scrub for their leaves and scratch back in relays. Their hardest work came when their contributions were piled at the base of the nest. The cock bird got to it first, his business-like beak swaying from side to side, his wide-awake eyes fairly shining, his long strong legs going like flails as he showered the leaves up in the air towards the crown of the nest. "What goes up must come down!" and some of the leaves and flying earth came showering back on his tail. He spared a hoarse, gasping cluck now and then as his mate showered her contribution up beside his. She did better for the little encouragement.

A brain-wave stopped me from shooting. Sometimes several, indeed many, turkeys used the one nest. Here was a nest that would yield eggs nearly every day for the collecting! So the two birds finished their job in peace. They stood a while panting with an up and down motion, then turned to gaze at one another, their brownish breasts puffed out, mutual admiration in their poise. Then the hen darted off into the. scrub. Immediately the male lowered his head and streaked after her. They had neither seen nor heard me. The hen just ran and the male chased her. In hungry anticipation I climbed up on that bulky soft stack, already in imagination filling my shirt with the white eggs buried below. I started digging in the centre of the flat crown. The leaves were fairly dry and lightly packed for the first foot in depth. Then came blacker, closer packed leaves that soon necessitated a tough stick to dig through. Quickly, warmth rose from that sodden mass. Digging deeper, the leaves were quite black and warm, almost caked: a trace of vapour drifted up from the hole. The eggs should not have been so deep as this, right down now in the belly of Nature's incubator! I sprang back in alarm as a bloated green centipede wriggled back among the leaves. Perspiring in that humid hole I widened it to a shaft and dislodged three sleepy green frogs wearing brown stripe bands, then an antediluvian beetle the width of a biscuit but half an inch thick, with long crooked legs all serrated and waving. His pitch-black body seemed sheathed in armour that creaked at the joints as he vainly struggled to escape. His head was terrifying-a death's-head skull with champing, menacing jaws. Natives had once shown me a similar beetle; so curiously, I pressed his abdomen hard. He roared! It was a tremendous sound from so small a bulk, but then the hideous old bluffer looked capable of a noise like a steam-roller.

Surprised and uneasy that the eggs should be so deep, I widened the edges of the hole and sighed. There lay exposed two eggshells, broken and dry! Then another broken shell; it had been a fresh egg too! Savagely I dug, but leaped gasping from the hole as a black snake hissed in it spitefully. His shining girth slid deep down among the leaves as, too late, I viciously stabbed down only to leap back at another commotion when the startled head of a scrub goanna poked up from the mould. He twisted back on the instant followed by the viciously poking stick. To a flurry somewhere outside I jumped up and peered over the crater edge just in time to see the goanna break out from the base of the nest and scurry away into the scrub.

He had allowed himself to be built right into the nest by the turkeys, while day by day he devoured their eggs. So intent on building their roof-garden were they that they had given no thought to the thief in the basement. Bitterly I wished he and the snake had fought it out to the death leaving me to carry the eggs to my hungry mates working and waiting away up the creek.

Emmargen Creek.

3

THE RUNAWAYS

ONE afternoon we knocked off work two hours earlier than usual, for the jungle grew ominously gloomy. As we trooped back towards camp, a dull rumble came and rolled away overhead. The sound, for some queer reason, actually trembled among the roots underfoot. The jungle was deathly quiet; not a call of a bird, not a movement of leaves, not even the dropping of quandong or plum; everything seemed waiting.

Charlie hurried to boil the billy before the storm arrived, while Norman and I lashed down the tent and cut a couple of extra props to support the galley. With the night the storm burst over the mountains. The trees "came" to us first; from far away they came sighing, then rapidly rippling, then howling as all bowed before the wind. As it roared down upon us the trees at the clearing edge shrieked to the grinding of their interlocked limbs. A branch snapped to whizz across the clearing sending our galley shed flying into the creek. We could "feel" the wind dragging and rolling among the treetops. The coals of the galley fire blazed furiously until blown in a dazzling spray out over the creek. Thunder broke to crash and grow I up and down the valleys. Rain fell in sheet after hissing sheet, pitting its downward strength against the speeding wind. We lay on our bunks in utter darkness, smoking, listening, waiting. Dragging crash after crash rumbled within the storm as some towering giant of the scrubs fell, bringing others in its fall.

We were afraid of the trees, those trees at the clearing edge with their crests writhing over our camp, their limbs connected by the swaying, hawser-like vines. If one tree came down, others must come! There would be no escape for us. While they stood they shielded the camp as a wall, but our ears strained above the wind to catch the ripping thumps should their roots give way. We would have sprung in a wild leap for the creek.

Before midnight the creek was "down," roaring past like a giant alive. Lightning flashed on writhing trees; sometimes the trunks lit up in flaming green to vanish in watery blackness. It was a terrible night.

I wondered what the wild things of the jungle were doing. Probably the animals had sought cubbyholes, the birds long since flown away, warned by that sense the wild things have of coming atmospheric trouble.

"There's something in here," said Charlie. "I can smell it!"

He struck a match, shielding it in cupped hands. We peered over the bunks.

"Goongarry!" came Norman's smiling voice. "He's lost his mother and has nowhere to go."

Two large, piteous eyes gazed up at us from a shivering bundle of wet fur; his little broad face was the picture of misery; his tail was his pride, but it dragged in the mud now. I laughed at his bedraggled ears as the match went out. It was a baby climbing-kangaroo. Charlie struck another match.

"There's a damn snake crawled in too!" he exclaimed with hostile emphasis.

"It's only a green tree-climber," said Norman as he leaned over his bunk, "it must have been blown down. Leave it alone or you'll scare the 'roo. See, he spots it and can look after himself."

The baby made a petulant dab with its forepaw at the glistening snake as it slithered under Charlie's bunk. We lay awake, smoking, listening, ready for that wild leap. How the waters would have washed us away!

During the early hours, the rain eased in fierceness, the wind ceased its whistling howl though still furiously swaying the treetops. Time must be close on dawn. It might be safe now to sleep. I rolled over, mind almost asleep, but that conscious subconscious part of it awake for the first warning screech of some belated tree.

"Stand! Don't move or I'll shoot!"

A low, beseeching growl answered Norman's steady command. It was a man's voice though it sounded like an animal's, and a strong animal odour filled the narrow tent.

Charlie's match showed a naked savage at the tent entrance with an apparently drowned girl clasped to his shaggy chest. As the match burned dim his eyes glared down upon the revolver, like a beast ready to run but imploring in fear.

"There's a candle butt under your bunk somewhere," said Norman.

Charlie rummaged for it and jerked back. "Hell!"

"What's wrong?"

"That slimy snake! I touched it!" He lit the candle, thrusting it up the neck of a broken bottle that was our lamp-glass. Under the feeble light we stared at our latest visitor. A young native, every inch a man, dumbly imploring our mercy; his face would have cried had it been made for tears. Norman nodded at the huddled burden.

"She was swept away when crossing the creek," he whispered in lingo. "Carried under a log – I could hardly find her!"

Charlie threw his blanket on the floor. They took the girl and stood her on her head vigorously rubbing her back and stomach until the water gushed out.

"Looks like she swallowed the whole creek," said Charlie. "Sling us your blanket, Jack."

They laid her on the blanket and massaged her limpness with quick, strong hands, while I worked her arms backwards and forwards. She was hardly fifteen years old, but a young woman to the native idea had she gone through their frightful initiation rites.

As she recovered consciousness, her large black eyes opened in fear, she struggled, gasping.

We held her while the man calmed her by looks and low, guttural words. She shrank back like a frantic animal.

We knew what it all meant. He had stolen her, with her consent as it proved. But – we saw she had not been through the Rite. And this meant death. He nodded dumbly to Norman's accusing eyes. And Norman sighed. (Did I explain that among the natives there is a sign language? Almost mental some of it is.) Norman looked inquiringly again, and the young man answered with expressive face and a lifting of the eyes. His voice was urgent with fear as he whispered:

"They follow fast – the Avengers!"

Again Norman looked the question with a working face. And again he answered so.

"Who is he?" asked Norman.

"Tarkooracoon!" he whispered, "the 'Nighthawk' – with six chosen warriors of the tribe."

I knew now that there was a man in the case apart from the far more deadly sin of stealing a girl who has not gone through the Rite.

Norman looked again and the native nodded, to burst out in distress:

"Yes, the Blood-oath!"

Then we knew that seven men had drunk each other's blood as a token to the tribe that they would never return until they hunted this man and woman to death.

"When did you take her?" inquired Norman.

"The night before last, but Tarkooracoon was watching – She was to have taken him the firestick soon!" (A token of betrothal.) "I had to run. But I doubled back and got the girl. They were on our tracks soon after-the Hawk sees in the night!"

"When did you enter the jungle side?"

"Last night."

"By the Spirit people, you travelled!"

"Death was following."

"But they could not see your tracks in the scrub."

"They carried pandanus torch!"

"They would not dare follow on into the jungle anyway; there was the night and the Spirits of the night-made mad by the storm! You have twelve hours start."

"Yes! But they travel like dogs on the scent of blood, knowing, too, I must cross the range by this way alone! With dawn they need not even seek our tracks until they come out on to the forest ahead."

Norman nodded.

"Still, you have twelve long hours start; that means life – if you rest! Lie down beside the girl and 'sleep in' the strength to run. The rain is ceasing, soon we light a fire and cook you food. The girl is done, but with strength in your limbs you can both go on – and live!"

The man dropped to his knees, sighing deeply. His eyes stared despairingly at his leg.

"He's wounded!" exclaimed Charlie as he bent" over the thorn-ripped thigh. "Got a spear-head in him!"

"There was a fight," the savage growled. Crouched in that tiny space we examined the wound. Luckily, it had been caused by a hunting-spear. He had broken off the spear-haft leaving the spear-tip and single hunting-barb in the wound. It was not a bad wound as native wounds go, but it must have put hell into the terror of that night, climbing the mountains through the wind-tortured jungle in fear of those Avengers coming behind, and with demons of superstition howling around him and the girl. Blood now was showing on her dried body where thorns and stakes had ripped the flesh.

The man lay like a collapsed log while Norman removed the spear-head. That sounds simple! It wasn't. Charlie held the light, hardly powerful enough to see the hairs on the limp leg. Luckily an inch of spear-point was protruding, while the broken-off portion of the spear-head was visible. They always take care to leave an inch of that. With a razor Norman slit up the flesh along the point (the swollen flesh to his practised eye showed the line of the barb) then pressed on the blade and steadily drew it down along the embedded barb almost to the point. This cut through the tough skin and into the flesh, then a deepening cut along the same line passed through the flesh and through the grass-tree resin and wallaby sinew which bound the barb to the point. The loosened barb was then prized out and the wound sluiced with Condy's to wash out chipped fragments of resin. Then little notches were cut along the protruding point and the end of a ribbon of tough rag neatly bound to it. (The notches would hold the rag from slipping.) Then Norman fastened his strong white teeth to the broken-off part, and pushed and twisted steadily, much as one pushes a tooth to loosen it. Then he pulled, moving his grip against the resistance of the flesh. I held the leg-it would surprise you what holding it took! As the broken spear-head was slowly withdrawn so the rag followed the point back through the wound, cleaning out any remaining cut materials which had bound the barb. The rag was then washed with Condy's and see-sawed through the wound several times while being splashed liberally with Condy's. A rough but efficient job, done surprisingly quickly. And the native never whimpered.

"We'll give it another go with Condy's," Norman said, "as soon as we've got boiling water."

Charlie rooted out what cooked tucker we had in the tucker-box. They just lay there and devoured the food like starving animals, the man with deep gratitude on his grim, heavy-brewed face; the girl like a child too terrified to be thankful.

She was quite shapely, as young lubras often are; her features were pleasing, too, despite the clay-daubed hair. Northern aboriginals have not the same thickness of nose and lips as those down south. A plaited grass-band still ornamented her arm, cut she dare not wear the plaited hair-belt of an initiated woman. She was dreadfully lacerated where thorns and come-back-quicks had torn the flesh. Her ears now were all for the jungle noises; she ceased eating in panting alarm at a shrieking moan outside. It was only the wind grinding one tree-branch against another but it shrieked a hellish "might be" to her.

Charlie reached under my bunk for some dry kerosene-tree wood, split it in the tent, then groped his way to the wrecked galley. The rain had ceased, the creek was roaring; the wind came in moaning waves of sound. Charlie soon had a fire going, with a fallen branch around it as a breakwind.

Charlie hurried the billy while Norman baked johnny-cake after johnny-cake and kept on baking them. Our visitors gulped the first billy of tea, then lay back sighing. It was a pleasure to put the billy on again, their eyes thanked us so.· The next billy went towards a dish of Condy's. I bathed the man's leg while Charlie reboiled the billy and brought in the first johnny-cakes. We opened some of our priceless tinned stuff, meat that we kept against a rainy day. Norman still kept on baking johnny-cakes. Fear-driven as they had been for two nights and days, those runaways ate like famished dogs.

The girl lay back heavy eyed, lips dreamily parted, looking absurdly childish. But the man grew restless with returning strength; he listened; his eyes rolled; he was "seeing" things.

"Sleep!" advised Norman firmly; "for three hours. Out in the forest it is only yet the breath of day. You will leave here after sleep, full bellied, fresh, and strong. They will arrive hours later, dead tired. You will be many miles away, carrying food, your bodies fresh. Give the girl a chance, and sleep to live. I promise to wake you! "

He gazed entreatingly at Norman, then his limbs relaxed and his eyes closed with a long, trusting sigh. In seconds almost, they were both dreaming heavily, dead to the world. They looked strangely different with the ruggedness and fear eased from their faces and limbs. She slept with an arm flung loosely across her warrior's neck.

He was a strong young chap, deep chested, lithely built. The usual incisor tooth had been knocked out; but we saw by tribal scars that he was still only a young warrior who had recently passed the second degree. A fillet of animal fur, adorned with claws and teeth, bound his coarse hair from a strong brow. His skin was a soft chocolate-brown, quite velvety looking after its night of thorough washing. A tomahawk, bound by an animal fur belt, fitted neatly against the small of his back. He had a taste for carving, as the deeply patterned zigzags upon his wommera showed. His spears were light hunting weapons; the heavier ones had been used apparently in that fight he mentioned. He appeared the sort of nigger who if he met a decent white man would stick to him through thick and thin. There are some like that.

We were in a quandary ourselves. If the avenging party suddenly turned up, Norman and Charlie would place themselves under a ban should they dare interfere in tribal laws, for they were "Group" as well as "Blood" brothers. Should I take the rifle and make a stand, the Avengers would be all around me behind the trees, at close spear-throw. Besides, the hunted people could hardly escape; they would be killed. If I did not meet the same fate, I would be a marked man by all the district tribes. And I wanted to do a lot of prospecting in that district yet.

Norman cooked two big piles of johnny-cakes, put three tins of meat and some tobacco and matches with each and made them into a handy bundle. The girl would carry it of course. Sharp at the three hours Norman woke them. The man instantly snatched his spears while the girl cowered at his feet.

"It is all right," soothed Norman. "Come and eat."

They crept to the fire, glaring around at the jungle. We bathed the man's leg again with Condy's and bandaged it while he drank hot tea, staring around at the trees, listening. The cat-bird frightened them cruelly when it imitated the tapping of a stone. As the girl gorged, her eyes roamed from tree to tree.

"Don't fear," reassured Norman. "Eat well, 'eat in' strength while you may!"

To her stare of horror the man sprang erect with poised spear as a bright little baby 'roo, in a shame-faced sort of way, scrambled from under the tent and after a shy peep towards us, half jumped, half hopped into the jungle.

We did not laugh, the man was trembling in every limb. He squatted down again with a sickly sigh.

"That reminds me," said Charlie grimly as he picked up a stick and poked under the bunk. But the snake had gone.

"Left without so much as a thank you!" smiled Norman.

The warrior grasped his weapons and stood erect, facing us, smiling. But it was the look in his deep-set eyes that thanked us. The girl picked up her bundle and stood by his side. Quite slight she looked, but gameness smiled out of her big black eyes.

The warrior grasped his wommera and with a guttural farewell turned and stepped swiftly away on the track that led up and out towards the forest. At the clearing edge the girl turned and smiled, then stepped into the jungle track.

We stood and listened for quite a while.

"They have a nine hours start," said Charlie.

"They will travel like hares."

"They will need to," answered Norman. "But they have eaten well; they carry food, and won't have to stop to search for it for the next five days at least."

"I hope they get away!" I said.

We knew that once they struck the forest they would turn sharp north, out into the wild forest lands. They would go nowhere near the haunts of the China Camp or Bloomfield tribes. With great luck they might break right through into the distant wild lands of the Mitchell. Once there, they would probably start a little nomad tribe all on their own. Throughout the ages, quite a number of Australian tribes must have originated in that way.

4

THE AVENGERS

WHEN would the Avengers come? About nightfall: we calculated. After climbing the range from away on the Daintree side, they would travel swift and fast through the jungle and across the mountain tops to our creek. There they would cross and come right past our tent. Grim men they would be too, an implacable party; none could turn them aside.

For the runaway had broken an implacable law; he had run away with an uninitiated girl. The penalty meant death for both.

The runaways belonged to Groups in which marriage was compatible, after initiation, providing relations were agreeable and the usual tribal etiquette observed. In this instance both were ignored, for immediately after initiation' the girl was to have been handed over to another man, Tarkooracoon the Night-hawk. That marriage had been arranged when the girl was a baby.

Had the girl been initiated when the lover ran away with her, then the couple, if they succeeded in eluding Tarkooracoon, could have returned to the tribe in a few months and taken their punishment. The lover would have had to face Tarkooracoon, and probably some of the Hawk's blood relations also. He would have been given a shield or wommera with which to defend himself, but no spears. If his skill and agility succeeded in warding off the spears of the aggrieved party, then probably all would be well. Tarkooracoon would have tried hard to wound but probably not kill him as a fatal conclusion would have led to inevitable feud, the lover's blood "brothers" being then bound to seek the life of the Hawk. With tribal honour thus satisfied, the Council of Old Men could decide as to whether the lover should keep the girl or not.

As to the punishment awaiting the girl, well – the women would have seized her, thrown her to the ground, and mutilated her with knives.

But the couple were to have no such way out.

For them the door was forever closed.

Smoking there by the remains of the galley, we discussed these intricacies of tribal law. The whole business is extraordinarily complicated, but all to a definite, closely-reasoned end. Their Group systems were thought out when humans are credited with having possessed only the reasoning power of monkeys. But the ancient men who thought out that system had brains. There is deep wisdom in the complete plan. It guards against intermarriage of blood relations, against the physically unfit, against cripples and hereditary disease and lunacy. It provides for the survival of the fittest and the breeding of the fit so that the tribe shall survive. We should not judge it by the awful initiation ceremonies. For some unknown reason that dread survival may even have been necessary. How can we judge man and the conditions which were necessary to his life in the prehistoric past?

It was too complicated a problem for Norman, Charlie, and me, so we stood up and stretched ourselves, glancing up the lane of trees down which was rolling the swift brown water of the creek. We were too sympathetic towards the runaways to sit there all day and wait for the Avengers, and yet it was impossible to occupy our minds with work while the creek was up.

We had to do something, so we followed the creek down towards a dull ceaseless thunder. As we walked we scanned the opposite bank, seeking swift travelling figures amongst the tree-trunks. Leaves and earth and roots were sloppy wet and slippery, a wompoo pigeon croaked hoarsely deep within the timber. The waters swept past high over the terrace banks, flattening down the undergrowth, dragging out the lawyer-canes into streamers of green ropes. Occasionally an uprooted tree swept by long swooping plunges to strike with a resounding crash against submerged boulders lining rocky bars.

We stuck to the steep edges of the spurs, sliding and slipping on the roots that ran like ridged mats down the creek-banks. Around the big bend, near where she plunged over the falls the thunder grew into a steady roar.

"It must be a great sight," shouted Charlie from the lead. "You'd think the water was tearing the mountain away. Look out you don't slip in or you're a goner!"

He slipped as he spoke, sliding down a slippery root, wildly clutching a creeper that snapped in a shower of leaves. He was under and gone in an instant, to bob up near the centre of the stream and strike out like the magnificent swimmer he is. He was swept down while swimming at an angle towards a bend where the bank curved in-stream. Below the bend was a bar of boulders; whirlpools marked the submerged danger.

Norman ran along the hilly bank taking no thought of risk, racing to reach the bend first and throw a lawyer-cane to Charlie who just could not reach the bank although his fingers just clutched the roots. He was sucked out-stream again and twisted under to shoot up just before the boulders, He heaved his weight out of the water to avoid striking, then plunged over in a porpoise dive. Half a minute later he bobbed up downstream striking out again for the bank. Around the bend he disappeared from view.

I panted after Norman shouting with a laugh that Charlie was. safe. There was now a long stretch of dragging water between him and the falls, but no more boulders. With distance in his favour he would make the water carry him to the bank quite easily. Any but a most cunning swimmer, however, would have had his head smashed upon that bouldery bar. We found him around the bend, sitting up on the roots pulling leeches from between. his toes. He smiled across at us and Norman laughed back.

Warily we crept along the tree-lined edge to near the falls. It was worth the risky walk. A spray of foam like a spinning cloud sprang up where the creek went over with a roar. We could not hear one another shout across the creek. Rock walls stood up each side of the falls and, held between them, a rainbow-tinted spray-cloud shut out the view beyond. As the stream approached the falls it ran on a slope, the silent water speeding with a frightening sucking motion. A splintered tree hurried along noticeably faster as it neared the falls, then went over like a swiftly moving match.

On our way back to camp we came on a tragedy of the night before-a fallen branch, from the hollow end of which drooped a dead mother, a queer little marsupial climbing thing, the size of a half-grown kitten. Its longish, furry tail was made like an opossum's for holding on to limbs; its claws were strong and hooked for climbing. From her pouch peeped a baby head. Mercy prompted us to kill the little orphan.

We had our evening meal very early, then Norman threw the burning wood into the creek leaving only one stick to smoulder and go black out. Charlie scraped out all our dry cut wood from under the bunks and hid it in the jungle. I said nothing, just went on smoking.

With the breath of night they came as we sat smoking around the ruined galley, seven ghostly figures stepping silently from the trees. They glared down at us, those naked figures in white pipeclay with a scarlet bar across each forehead. Their bodies smelt loathsomely of rancid human oil. Even the tropic storm, the fording of river and creeks, could not wash that smell away. Each carried war spears, cruel long things with a three-foot spear-head barbed with spikes of bone. Their blood-shot eyes, their indrawn lips, their lean flanks told of a stern, famished chase. These almost tireless human hounds would travel until they dropped; not until their sinews numbed would they turn aside to seek food that they might hurry on again.

All were warriors past the third degree, proud of the mutilations that proved them so; each wore the feather and the phallic emblem. More ominous still was that brand of the killer on their grim, hostile faces.

Without asking we knew him, for Tarkooracoon, the Night-hawk, stood out from his fellows. A nose like a curved beak projected between a devil's eyes, his set mouth was a sneer. His corrugated brow was blood-clotted from the tear of a come-back-quick; the sinews of his spear-hand twitched on the wommera as he glared at Norman.

Norman nodded.

"How long?" gutturally demanded the Hawk.

"In the middle of the night," answered Norman. "They travelled fast. They ate here then pushed on through the storm. Long before dawn they would be far out in the forest country. And now the night has come. Camp here. We will cook you food and you will be fresh tomorrow."

"We will have the food – now," sneered the Hawk. "We will have them – tomorrow!"

It took Norman a long time to find a stick of dry wood. When he did so he had to chop it all in little pieces, finally he had to scrape around for kindling to start it burning, and he didn't succeed in lighting it properly without a lot of blowing. The Avengers squatted down, frowning at his efforts. Charlie produced some nigger-twist tobacco and gravely handed it round. Each man accepted his share, broke it in pieces with his thumbs, and rolled coarse cigarettes in strips of an old *Bulletin.* They lit up with a firestick and puffed clouds of coarse smoke in a famished enjoyment .

They would not talk, only grunt an answer – which is a way Avengers have. I disliked the brutes while realizing that they were quite justified, according to their own laws and their own way of thinking. The runaways had been condemned to death by the collective order of the Council. The Hawk snarled a mirthless smile as he grunted this decree of the Old Men. And we knew that it meant he could batter his rival to death without fear of a blood feud.

Norman was very slow mixing up the flour, and when he had done so, found there were hardly any coals. In a flurry of aggravated swear words he built up the fire anew. At last he flattened out the johnnies and laid them on coals that were nearly black. He was bending to turn them when the Hawk grunted harshly and snatched one off the coals. His courteous comrades did likewise, flicking off the charcoal then ramming the uncooked things down their throats. One man's teeth were worn nearly to the gums through years of grinding on ashes, sand, and bone.

As Norman mixed up more johnnies the Hawk's eyes rolled ominously, his teeth gritted not so much on charcoal as with suppressed rage. His men were famishing! This had promised to be a meal with no waste time. It was very slow and-the prey was escaping – with the seconds.

The Hawk and his friends were middle-aged savages, all lithely built, with chests, shoulders, and backs heavily cicatriced, their sullen faces deeply lined. All wore moustaches; two wore a bone through the cartilage of the nose.

These were terrible pursuers to be on a man's track; muscle and sinew trained to the limit of human endurance, capable of outstaying many an animal. Eyes that could follow the flight of a bee, see the stub of a toenail in the bark of a root, detect the "ghost" imprint of a bare foot upon a bare rock, and in open country distinguish anything moving miles away.

Impossible for any who understand to be contemptuous of these men. They looked on civilized man and the civilized man's life and ideals with contempt. Had they been chasing a civilized man he would have been dead long ago.

The Hawk was no outraged rival in love. He had never loved the stolen girl; she was his by the right of bargain. His fierce joy now was to catch the runaway and knock out her brains. The Avengers were out after blood because two lovers had offended against tribal law. That the girl happened to have been the Hawk's merely added pleasure to the job of killing her and the lawless lover.

The Hawk snatched a last johnny-cake and grabbing his spears sprang up, grunted to Norman, and with noiseless strides disappeared up the path. The others followed, vanishing like ghosts in the night.

Norman and Charlie smoked seriously as we gazed out at the black jungle.

"What are the lovers' chances?" I asked at last.

"Even," answered Norman musingly. His handsome face was even nicer in its sympathy. "They have a start that counts," he went on softly. "They had sleep and food. Once out in the forests and they will wade down a creek in the effort to lose their tracks; then hurry on until they drop. But it all depends on the girl. He will never leave her. It all depends on how long she can keep travelling."

5

"BIG-NOSE"

HOWEVER, the rules and regulations of native life were no concern of ours, so on this as on other occasions we minded our own business by seeking that elusive gold.

"It's hard to find," said Charlie, "but it does not mean the Bone."

"Pointing the Bone," was a nasty habit of the old witch-doctors. It meant death to the native menaced. It might not act against the white men, but in their case, a spear from the scrub could do the trick.

Those jungle trips of ours were grand. Life was glorious. One felt one would never grow old. I remember how once we laughed, in civilization, when a greybeard assured us we would surely grow old.

However, man cannot live by meat alone; the longing for flour, jam, and "Cocky's joy" craves satisfaction. So when our last johnny-cake was eaten we would lash the tent-poles against wind and rain, tie up the tent sides so that inquisitive pig or cassowary could not push right through it, roll our blankets, and start out on the joyous walk to the Bloomfield. Charlie would soon be out of sight along the jungle path, Norman striding effortlessly over the interlaced roots and lawyer-canes, dodging the slippery fall-aways of fern-covered ravines. And there was always a song in our hearts.

Leeches were a pest if the ground leaves were shining after rain. When crossing the tangled morass at any creek-head we would see the crawlers stretched upward on many a dead leaf, their heads twisting, their india-rubber necks swaying as they waited; some even hurried towards us over the leaves. The instinct of these bloodsuckers is uncanny. Whether they smelt, heard, or saw I don't know; possibly they were delicately sensible to the vibrations from our feet. Though we swathed our boot-tops in soaped rags, the slimy pests would squeeze down into the boots, stretch in between the cloth and worm up our legs, fasten on, and bloat themselves with blood. When the burning itch and sting became unbearable we each would whip off a boot, hurriedly strip the leg of the slimy black mass, jerk the clingers off, tip the bloaters out of the boot, then thrust in the bloody leg; whip off the other boot, repeat the performance, and be quick and lively on the march again before a whole army of leeches closed in. Only after heavy, or during the light, incessant rain, were the leeches bad. At other times we would not get a dozen on us in a mile walk.

Charlie always led. I followed Norman, gloating at the thought of the feed awaiting us in China Camp. Just as eagerly we looked forward to the forest and the sky. Our eyes used to hunger for the open country as our appetites did for other food.

It was glorious. We would step out of the jungle on to a forest peak clothed with bloodwood and ironbark, with grass all agleam and waving in the mountain breeze. There was, too, always a bird calling here, whereas "inside" was so often hushed. The sunlight in the open forest gleamed dazzlingly after the gloom of the scrub. From our feet, the world dropped far away. Like a cow's tongue licking a far-away hillside we could see the red gash that was Lode Hill, monument to the indomitable determination of Jack Elliott. Across the great valley but to the right towered the huge bulk of Mount Alexander and the crown of Peter Botte with its "Two Sisters" – a landmark to mariners far out at sea. The natives tell a sinister legend of those two crouching rock-masses upon the wind-blown peak.

We would thankfully sit on the grass for a spell, taking off our boots for a final clean out of leeches. The pests are not often found in the forest country; there they are a different kind and far less numerous. Sometimes a butterfly would come fluttering along. One day a snow-white one perched palpitating on Charlie's coal-black hair.

"It is the soul of a little native girl," he smiled.

Charlie was always the first to leap up and hurry whooping down our forest pad.

Sometimes a flash of black and gold would streak overhead as a rifle-bird sped into the scrub. The deceptive green wall to the right shielded "Christy's Pocket," a few acres of grass walled in by scrub. The Bairds could never pass by without telling me some new story of that noted law-breaker, yet friend to the needy, the northern Queensland Robin Hood. Those few acres of sweet forest grass were his hideout, in which he could secrete his beloved horses and himself. In Palmerston's day, Robert Baird had started a store for the Chinese gangs and "tin-scratchers" farther along towards the Meg at China Camp. And it was back to this hidden Pocket that a trusted emissary of Baird's used to hasten with the news that the police had come.

Thrilling stories, many authentic, are told of this noted explorer, bushman, and one-time fugitive from justice. He was a strange character; fiercely reckless, yet with a cold reasoning behind all his actions. Undoubtedly warm of heart yet keeping coldly aloof from his fellow men, and living in scrub and jungle as if a blood-brother of the animals and trees.

He had discovered a pass across the mountains which he never revealed to others. I suspect our Daintree pass was it. Though troopers, in pursuit of Christy, might ride night and day to get round the mountains, he would vanish almost at their touch and two days later be in country they had left a week before.

In districts where Christy was known his name calls up mystery and romance with stories of sudden death softened by warm-hearted deeds. He would help a lonely settler, a sick mother, and disappear as silently as he had come, declining thanks with a cold moroseness that chilled the thanker. Deeds of another sort he carried out as swiftly and disappeared as silently. Across on the Cairns-Atherton side, among the old-timers there, his name is still almost worshipped. While on the Cooktown side they say there can never be another Christy Palmerston.

He was a real mystery man. No one knew who he was, from whence he came, nor where he would go. The closest white friend he ever made was Robert Baird. Christy lived for long periods in the dense scrubs with a faithful blackboy (a noted boy) his only company. At periods in his earlier career he had quite a bodyguard that followed him like black panthers. To see him thus step from the jungle, lithe and sinewy, with brown beard and piercing eyes, is a picture printed indelibly on the minds of men who saw the sight. He has gone straight through a township with his bodyguard trailing after him while the people came out to stare, eager to lend a hand if he asked- but only if he asked.

The government of the day, faced with great pioneering difficulties in opening up a distant country of mountain, jungle, and scrub, recognized the value of this man with his uncanny jungle instinct. He was offered a job at work he might love; his transgressions (if any) to be wiped out. Would he find a track from the inaccessible tableland ranges down to the Mourilyan and thus open up the rich lands on the tableland for settlement? He did. Soon he was recognized as a government official of the highest ability. His work was almost always that of the path-finder, opening up tracks through jungle and scrub, connecting one settlement with another, and piercing farther into country which has since become part of northern Queensland's richest sugar lands.

In these latter years of his life Christy entirely changed, although he always remained a remarkably quiet man. He led two lives, that of the wild scrub man of his earlier days, and that of the kindly civilized man, undertaking any hardship to help his fellow man and country. He married, and was a beloved husband and father. People who knew him well in both "lives" tell fascinating stories of his unique career.

The Baird boys naturally remembered more vividly those stories connected with Christy and their father around the district in which they were born. On the Atherton-Cairns-Mourilyan side Christy was better known as the path-finder, and helper of lonely ones, then the great-hearted government official. While on the Cooktown side the old hands fairly gloated on tales of him in the wild Palmer days, in savage fights between black and white, in stories of Hell's Gate, Battle Camp, and Death's Pass, in the bloody fights of the Chinese factions, in tales of gold and the carrying of it through the lonely places, and in dare-devil rides by day and night through scrub and forest, over river, mountain, and plain.

Those were the Palmer days, when it cost an ounce of gold and a fight to win a kiss from "Palmer Kate," queen of distant Cooktown. At that time the Palmer country (a long way from our "country") swarmed with bands of armed whites. Then, twenty thousand Chinamen toiled for gold on the Palmer, and won it in tons-not ounces. Cooktown harbour had to find berth for a competitive fleet of vessels of all nations. The roaring town never slept day or night. It is a pity those days would not come again, even at the cost of another two thousand Chinamen and a few score of whites being eaten by the natives. "'Tis an ill wind that blows nobody any good."

Norman and Charlie were always greeted as kings by the China Camp tribe, greeted in dignified fashion by the old men first, then the warriors, then the young bucks. Some of the old chaps had eaten Chinamen; several could tell what a white tasted like. Those feasts had lingered in their memories. On fitting occasions the epicures loved to discuss them – but never before a white man unless he was deeply trusted. Chinaman makes the tenderest "long pig" so they assured me: he is juicy too. White man's flesh, though agreeable, is rather salty. Blackman's flesh is the toughest; young girl in good condition being the tenderest.

These people, however, even in their hectic days were not often cannibals in the strict sense of the term. They ate human flesh only occasionally and then generally in relation to a tribal custom, or to imbibe the cunning, strength, or fighting qualities of the victim. On rare occasions the reason was definitely cannibalistic, as when they attacked a party and ate the killed.

Christy Sorenson and Johann Scogstrom were great old battlers of those parts. We generally pulled up at Johann's for the first meal. Johann had built a little house by a creek among banana and papaw trees. He was a plump little chap with a quiet smile. Far more interesting, he was a scrubman: he would disappear for months prospecting in the scrubs. The natives carried for him. He was deeply sympathetic towards them and helped them out of troubles with the whites and far distant officialdom. A thoughtful, understanding man, he had delved into native mentality.

The whites in that isolated little camp were mostly wages men, working for the Lode Hill and Roaring Meg Tin Mining Companies. From the little huts dotted distantly down the hillslopes, they always welcomed us cheerily and hastened to put the billy on for the "Wild Men of the Scrubs." Had we not come from the mysterious jungle scrub? Were we not looking for gold?

No one knew when we might drop on it! Even in that small isolated community rumour was rife concerning certain little yellow pieces we had found. I believe gold whispers its own tidings.

How we enjoyed those civilized meals! There were no luxuries: the appetite that fights to build a young body was luxury enough. All food had to come from Cooktown thirty odd miles to the Bloomfield by pearling lugger, then on packhorses nearly twenty miles. So the China Camp men had no *pate de foi gras* or pickled oysters to place before their guests. But damper, tinned butter, jam and perhaps cheese, were the acme of luxury to us.

Several days later we would be whistling along the deep-red pack track to the Bloomfield, our ears alert to distinguish hum or roar. We were relieved when a distant, sullen hum told us that the Roaring Meg was not "up." Wading that ice-cold stream, the current viciously dragging us towards the swirling rapids only a few yards lower down, was always a nervy job. The quiet, white grave-stones on the opposite bank did not help a man either.

Here we crossed the turn-off to the Scrub Camp perched up in the mountains close by the headwaters of the Roaring Meg, but on the seaward side. The Scrub Camp was even more isolated than China Camp. Some wild and woolly tales of fact could be written of the Scrub Camp. .

Up there they were either "working mates," or "on his own." A warm-hearted crowd; some a bit tough. Bitter feuds have been fought out there. The Scrub Camp incurred the wrath of Nature occasionally. During the wet season a cyclone would now and again rage in from the sea and howl into the mountains piling up the trees like scythed grass. The heart of a cyclone clears its own "track." One such track was marked by uprooted and splintered tree-trunks, piled in places twenty feet high, that ran for miles across the mountain tops.

When past the turn-off to the Scrub Camp, our track meandered along a forest divide, winding for miles, with timbered ridges and steep gullies to either side. Occasionally Norman would lead me to the edge of a spur and point down to a rock-lined gully-head, upon which the blacks had lain, peering between the grass-tufts with spears gripped between their toes, worming their way along and ever up the spur as they listened to the coming hooves, waiting for a party of prospectors travelling along the ridge above. It was intensely interesting, listening to a man to whom as a "blood-brother" the natives had shown the secrets of all their ambushes, explained their plans, and discussed the reason why. Very cleverly had the black men arranged their numerous forays against white, yellow, and black. If they had only been a little less fearful of the assumed superiority of the whites, they would have played havoc among the few scattered men of the Peninsula.

Finally we would come to the zigzag to twist and turn and twist again down to the beautiful Bloomfield, tranquilly flowing between hill and mountain, through grassy forest and dense green scrub. Dull green mangroves lined its mouth, tall coconut-palms the upper reaches right to the lovely falls.

We always stayed at Pierce's Landing, a shed and a slab hut built on a high bank overlooking a southern stretch of the river. In that district, China Camp, walled in by mountains, is the end of the world. The only way out is the track to the Bloomfield, then across Wyalla Plain, up Stucke's Gap and across the Romeo Mountains to Cooktown – a lonely but exceedingly beautiful eighty-mile track. So the rare travellers, who came to or went from the Bloomfield had to ford it at Pierce's Landing. Every four or more months, as God, sea, or rainy season willed, the little supply-lugger would arrive from Cooktown and anchor in the river-mouth. Next day, like a toy ship with furled sails upon a river of liquid glass she would be towed upstream, hill and mountain echoing to the song of the coloured rowers. Then Arthur and Albert Pierce with their big pack-teams and native stockmen, would load up and pack the stores to the two hungry mining-camps in the mountains.

On this particular trip of ours, there were no stores awaiting us at the Landing. A waterside dispute was on somewhere in the outside world. It was no business of ours, but the trouble kept us without civilized food for four months. Later, a similar trouble delayed us.

However, we loved the Bloomfield, so we sat down happily to wait. The Pierces grew bananas, "sweet buks," manioc, sour-sops, granadillas, and pumpkins in their garden; fish were in the river; pigeons, turkeys, and pigs in the scrub. So what did we care!

The following morning, I renewed acquaintance with old Big-nose. Just a peep, as he cunningly skirted the mangrove shadows on the opposite side of the river. Not a ripple from the tip of his long snout as he drifted downstream with the current. All that one could see was the snout tip, the horny ridge of his eyes, then, behind ten feet of water, the serrated ridges of his tail just moving to steer him clear of the bank. He sank without a ripple before he came opposite the Landing. Well he knew the danger. Someone was always there ready for a pot-shot at any unwary alligator.

All northern Queensland calls these treacherous reptiles "the 'gator," or "lizard." They are really the estuarine crocodile; and our north breeds the fiercest and largest in the world. One, shot in the Pioneer River, measured thirty-two feet from tip to tip. But the one that "Anzac" Bennet shot in the Endeavour River must, by its barrel-like bulk, have measured more. It taped over twenty feet with more than half of its tail missing-bitten off in some submarine battle.

The long jaws of our crocodile have from fifteen to twenty conical teeth on each side of both jaws. From the tip of the snout, air passages run back to its throat, a thoughtful provision of nature which enables it to drown its prey and breathe at the same time. A great fourth tooth on each side of the lower jaw adds to the croc's frightfulness. These fit into notches on the upper jaw. When it gazes at you from the mud around the mangrove roots, the first things you are aware of are the terrible eyes and those horrible teeth. Just so you invariably become aware of a boar by his eyes and tusks. In the true alligator, you cannot see these teeth when the mouth is closed. Further, the alligator is smaller and far more sluggish than our fightable beast.

Apparently the reason why Queensland bushmen called our crocodile an alligator was became of the. Johnstone River crocodile, a little chap growing to six and seven feet. He is really a freshwater "lizard." The natives love to eat it and the innumerable eggs the female lays. This crocodile is not very dangerous. I have seen natives swimming in a lagoon while the crocodiles scurried from their antics. All the same, I noticed that only the strongest swimmers acted the "flash fellow," and they were pretty lively too when diving amongst the frightened reptiles. The swimmers made a great commotion vociferously echoed by the remainder of the stick-throwing tribe on the lagoon banks.

However, up north we are so used to calling the sea-going crocodile an alligator that I'll call him so here.

The Pierce brothers as usual were very annoyed with the Bloomfield alligators. They had lost several valuable horses and more cattle since our last visit. The reptiles (old Big-nose in particular) would lurk at a pool chosen by the animals for drinking, and wait close up under the bank with a patience only equalled by a Chinaman awaiting his vengeance. A week after arriving at the Bloomfield I saw with an awful helplessness, Big-nose tackle a little roan filly.

6

THE LURKING TERROR

IT was just at sundown. My bank of the river was lined with dark green scrub, while opposite, the water mirrored the graceful palms. Behind me the hills rose steeply right from the water's edge. From the black falls up-river a murmurous volume of sound rolled down. I carried no rifle, for Charlie had taken it pig-shooting with the natives, and the Pierce brothers had taken theirs into the bush seeking a beast. Norman was miles away down the river.

I pushed out from the shrubbery on to a jutting ledge of rock where the water looked dark and deep, an ideal fishing-pool. At a sharp hoof-click against a stone I looked across the water and saw the little roan filly coming down through the solitary scrub-patch opposite. Cattle had broken a pad through the undergrowth there to the one shallow waterhole, and along this came the filly, her steps hesitant, ears twitching nervously, nostrils distended. She edged down the sloping bank but stood well back from the water's edge, peering in big-eyed anxiety. It looked an innocent pool, and was a favourite drinking-place of cattle. But the filly was timid: perhaps she had received a fright there. She advanced a step with lowered head, peering into the water. Though the water was shallow the bank appeared just a little undermined.

At last the filly ventured, evidently thirsty. Standing well back she stretched her muzzle to the water. Even then she did not drink; fearfully she stared, her nostrils quivering, ready to bound away. Finally she drank, slowly at first, then deeply, at last in gulping confidence. The long snout of Big-nose thrust up, and, gripping her nose, almost dragged her straight in with that first wrenching pull. An awful struggle followed as she wrenched back against the weight of the alligator, her eyes bulging, her body arched as she strove to lever herself backwards. Her hooves crunched the bark from the roots, her tail wedged between her legs, and her mane ruffled stiffly in terror. Those fangs buried in her nose choked every whimper. Her muscles tautened violently, her ribs stood out as she wrenched in frantic straining. With convulsive strength she almost lifted the brute from the water. His massive grey back and chest was a hideous weight as his claws sank into her shoulders ripping the flesh to ribbons; then his bulk thumped back with a splashing whouff! whouff! as he used his weight while wrenching his head as a dog does when dragging a wallaby to the ground. Back-paddling, tugging with his snout, swirling his tail for leverage he twisted her head to the very roots while both made coughing, gasping, wheezing sounds. Under that awful strain she grew appreciably smaller, shrank within herself. As inch by straining inch she began to give way her struggles grew all the more terrible, her slipping hooves wedged deeper between the roots.

Foiled in that first swift pull, he tried to drag her muzzle under. He could breathe with his mouth full of muddy water; hers was crushed in his snout. He thrust her back upon her haunches as his chest heaved upwards only to surge back, then heave up and wrench down again. I hurled stones in a shouting helplessness as bitter as that terrible fight opposite. As the filly weakened her body nearly overbalanced, her straining legs appeared ready to snap. Then he swirled his bulk almost side on and tugged as his gorilla-like forepaws snatched at the bank for leverage while his great tail whipped up over the bank. The hammer-like blow echoed as the broken-legged filly came tumbling into the river. Even then she struggled in choking agony against being dragged under, while his submerged body clawed and tailed its way backwards along the bottom. Presently only the hind-quarters of the filly were visible, wobbling in feeble tremblings. In deep water his weight dragged her down to the depths.

Everyone liked Arthur and Albert Pierce; queer opposites, except in their slight physique. Arthur was inclined to be ginger, with blue eyes. Bert was dark, with moustache and eyes to match. Arthur was quiet, a great worker, but a dreamer when times were slack. Bert was one of the rowdiest men I have ever met and a favourite with the blacks, who called him "Chulbil." We seldom called him anything else, and he really did have something of the goanna's snappy liveliness to make the name stick. Arthur avoided the natives except in the ordering of their work; Chulbil was overflowing with lively spirits and health. Arthur, often racked with malaria, would be quietly planning for that long-dreamed-of lugger while Chulbil's carefree laugh echoed from the river or came yodelling down from the zigzag.

But both men hated Big-nose. They were out to get him. Always a native would be watching the river crossing by day, while in early morning and at sundown one of the brothers, rifle in hand, would step into the timber lining the riverbank, or paddle quietly upstream in the dinghy, sneaking round the bends to peer at the mudbanks exposed at low tide. One morning on a mudbank something white glistened in the early sunrise. Wallowing tracks were fresh in the mud. That something was the skull of a native, with a shin-bone sticking up from the mud.

Big-nose was the present menace. No doubt when he was shot, another would arise, as has always happened on the river. But Big-nose was now a menace to Olufson's youngsters. From up-river, round the bend, they had to row a good five miles downstream to the tiny school. Big-nose had taken to following them, his snout-tip visible a hundred yards behind the dinghy. He would join them every morning as they rounded the bend and follow them right to school. An elder sister rowed the youngsters down, brought the dinghy back, and re turned for them in the afternoon. The regular rhythm of rowlocks coming and going was a familiar sound at the Landing. Each day, Big-nose made his appearance just a little closer to the dinghy. When the dinghy stopped, he stopped; when it rowed on again, he followed. The youngsters piled stones in the dinghy and when the thing glided within range they pelted him, shouting their childish insults regarding the shameful history of the alligator family as detailed by the coloured youngsters at school.

Thereafter the alligator followed just out of range, his snout-tip, the horny rims above his eyes, the ridges of his tail following effortlessly in the wake of the dinghy. Then Olufson rowed to school -with a rifle. But Big-nose did not appear. He didn't appear for a week and the busy father again trusted the children to the elder sister. The youngsters had not seen the cunning alligator for some time now. But the river folk are wise to the ways of the alligator.

An intensely interesting settlement is the Bloomfield. Our busy cities, their interests mainly centred in the life of the city, might find it hard to believe that such places exist in Australia. The remote mountain river with its tiny colony of whites, coloureds, and natives. The Olufsons' home up the river below the Falls. (Past the Falls was the uninhabited land.) Olufson and his splendid wife were the last word in pioneers. He was a blue-eyed, bearded chap with the blood of Vikings in his veins. He had carved out a home there right at the end of the world. Despite floods and blacks, loneliness and isolation, he had made his home self-supporting.

That large busy family grew and made practically everything they needed, and they lived well too. They made their own flour from corn when needs must, candles and soap and household things the girls made too.

The mother had educated her capable daughters into quiet, nice-mannered young women. Educated them, too, so that when the inevitable call to civilization came they would be able to take their places in competitive commercial life. One of the many grim experiences of the mother was a tree falling on her husband. That is why he is lame. She had to chop the tree from off him.

I met many wonderful women up north, and used to wonder what would be their reward. Perhaps they looked for it in their children. I think they deserve something more.

Two miles downstream from Olufson's, on the opposite bank, was Pierce's Landing. A few miles downstream again, amongst the frangipanni was old Philip Johnson's; and a quarter mile farther along, the palm-clustered house of old Antonio, perched upon tall piles on the hillslope above the bank. Opposite was the river island, echoing with native life, always the howl of a dog, shrill chatter of lubras, yells of piccaninnies. Sometimes the muffled reverberation of a hollowed log, the drumming of thighs, the sullen stamp of feet.

Lower down still was Georgie Osmundson's place with the *Pearl Queen* at anchor in front of the house and dark green hills rising sheer behind. Where the slopes of the steep hills had been cleared of timber with their binding roots, the wet seasons had taken vengeance in the shape of deep red scars-landslides that threatened at any "wet" to rush down upon the little houses and sweep them into the river.

Across the river opposite, on the flat which stretches miles back and broadens into Wyalla plain, was the coloured settlement: little houses surrounded by shady mangoes, papaws, five-finger, and custard-apple trees. Granadilla vines draped the verandas bright with croton and hibiscus. In behind the dull green mangroves that line the riverbank there, was visible the light green of the banana palms, and gardens of sweet-buk and manioc. The predominant types were families of Malay and Islander. But South Sea men were there too, and when a couple of Jap pearlers called in, the settlement would be lively with big-footed, woolly-headed Papuans in their lava-lavas, and roamers from the Coral Sea. Some of the mixtures, especially the feminine ones, were of entrancing interest. The blood of whites, Chinese, and unnamed eastern races was represented in that little population of hospitable, passionate, sullen, laughing, fiery people.

The coloured people lived in families – sometimes groups of families. Several families owned or shared a *bêche-de-mer* lugger or cutter. In the season most of the men would be away "outside" for months at a time fishing, either in the co-operative vessel or as a signed-on seaman among the northern pearlers. During the cyclone, the "lay-up," season all vessels sailed home and the Bloomfield seafarers came back laden with good things from Port. The following three months were merry indeed. During the other nine, the families at home had to live to a large extent on what their gardens produced. The river was navigable only for small craft for about eight miles upstream.

Walking back up-river from the settlement, one comes to the tiny schoolhouse, where white and coloured youngsters mix and learn queer things not in the curriculum. The things they should learn were then taught by a quaint, white-haired old schoolmaster. Next, was Mrs Ayres's cottage-tall widow with the many goats and big heart. Big sons, too; one is now a giant of a man. Then came the long shady track among the trees high up on the winding riverbank, right back to Olufson's. Through those trees one caught glimpses of the river, like slowly rolling silver. But when the Roaring Meg came tumbling down, the Bloomfield would be a sullen, hurrying brown. On one such morning Norman stepped smiling into the shed.

"Come out and watch one of your friends surf-bathing, Jack," he said in that soft voice of his. "Be quick, before Chulbil gets the rifle."

Coming downstream, playing with a rolling log, was Big-nose, in the exuberance of his fun forgetting all about the danger at the Landing. He would swirl back from the log, allow it a spinning start in the current, then with one swish of his tail be up to and over it, submerging it under his bulk. He dived, came up beside it and straddled it, rolling it over and over under his chest then dived head first over it with a great show-off of his hind-quarters. Some instinct must have warned him, for he vanished the instant that Chulbil came running with the rifle.

Arthur Pierce was a born pioneer though cursed with recurrent attacks of malaria. When a lad, he had worked as stockman up in the lonely Peninsula, and while there had taught himself to read and write. Then he trekked down here with his savings and a few horses. Now he had bred some hundreds of horses; did all the packing to the two mining-camps; and had taken up a big slice of that forest country which he was gradually stocking with cattle. All in the course of a very few years. He planned now to buy the supply-lugger and do all the "shipping" to the Bloomfield.

A couple of years later he had realized this step in his dream. What was more he taught himself seamanship and navigated the craft, signing on a native crew. In slack times he left his brother to manage their interests at the Landing while he took the vessel out to the Barrier Reef, and learnt all about *bêche-de-mer*, how to dive for, cure, and sell it. So that he would lose no time by the vagaries of the wind, he later installed an engine and taught himself mechanics.

Wyalla is a plain of tangled grasses traversed by tree-shaded creeks and dotted with occasional low hills, all hemmed in by big dark mountains. This plain has been for ages a fighting-ground of the aborigines; and here a white man has led them in battle. Hundreds of warriors, ochred and befeathered, brandishing their huge, painted shields, stamping the earth in the growing frenzy of fight, have roared their war-cry behind that haranguing chief who led them on, he the wildest of the wild.

He has sat as chief in their councils, has taken the lead in their corroborees, their hunts, their life; he has worn the eagle-hawk feather; and a belt of human hair has adorned his savage thighs. He has sat within the gunyahs of the people, has sung by their campfires, has been one of them.

Well-educated man, yet chief of a group of tribes, with the power of life and death in his hands, he has led a wonderful life. He lives and sighs, for he has seen his warriors scattered to but a remnant of their former glory.

Just below the Landing on the edge of a scrub-patch were the gunyahs of a branch tribe who supplied recruits as stockmen to the Pierce brothers. They were a mercurial little crowd, just like the big tribe downstream on the island. Some days we would hear their camp ringing with laughter, the youngsters playing at "March Fly" (the boy chasing the girl to buzz in her ear and pinch her stomach) the shrieks of the girl encored by the lubras as they sat pounding zamia nuts or weaving dilly-bags. Smiling men teaching the toddlers how to track lizards, mothers laughing at babies that sprawled and kicked and crooned in the sun. The next day the camp would be queerly silent with the people squatting by their gunyahs sullen and morose, not even the blowing of a leaf-blade or the tapping of a wommera. But the following day would see normal life again, the chatter of the women, the spear-making of the men, the piccaninnies playing at gunyah building and "being married," the infernal music enthusiast blowing hoarsely and monotonously on the yiki-yiki. A tame cassowary and wallaby solemnly followed this crowd in their periodical "walk-abouts" through the bush.

Pets had a rough time though. Occasionally the bucks would bring in a young bird or baby wallaby, laugh with the piccaninnies at the unfortunate thing's antics and fear of the dogs, only to quickly tire of it and leave it to the children. These would tie a string around the unfortunate creature's neck and drag it about the camp until a dog snatched it away. A well-developed captive that clung doggedly to life, they would tie to a stick and leave it to fight starvation and the dogs.

Those people are very interesting, but they live in another world really; a rather dreadful place at times it would be to us.

Our conversation often was in "lingo." Norman, Charlie, and Chulbil, could speak it as well as the natives. Arthur refused to learn it, but I did, not liking to be in with the crowd and yet out of all the jokes. But I learned just sufficient to carry on with. It is an invaluable acquisition to a man if he is working in native country, or if studying them. He cannot learn without it. But remember, you who may be interested: there is a "secret" language as well, rarely explained to a white man. The trouble is that when a man moves on he has to learn all over again, should he be sufficiently interested. A tribe only thirty miles away might not understand one word of the lingo you know.

We were gossiping one dark night when the river took on an unearthly beauty. Up with the tide floated a lake of lovely but eerie colours, like a cloud of dancing, iridescent, green and red phosphorescent light. We watched it as it floated past. Apparently that pool of brilliance was a mass of phosphorescent animalcules or plant-life that had come up from the ocean. A big fish sped through it like a streak of molten gold and green. As he twisted and turned chasing his prey he seemed to set the river on fire.

Harry Watson (left) and friends with a Plains Turkey and two wild boar, shot at Gregory Downs Station, Queensland 1917.

7

THE "KILLER OF PIGS"

ONE afternoon early I rowed across the river from the Landing, tied the dinghy by the hole where the alligators lurk to catch horses crossing at low tide, and walked down the tree-lined path leading towards the settlement. When three miles down, curiosity or luck lured me off the track, across a sunlit forest pocket and into a shady patch of unfamiliar scrub. Insects hummed busily in the cool air lit by filtered sunlight: a dragonfly sped by on scarlet wings. Hardly any undergrowth hid the beauty of the tall, slim trees and one could avoid the vines and walk easily among them. It was a dreamily peaceful spot. I filled the pipe and gazed around, enjoying the beauty of it all. A bird called in low sweet tones; it was easy to sense the message in its song. Presently a tinkling splash suggested someone washing clothes.

There in a clearing the fairies might have made gleamed two tiny pools, the larger rimmed with white sand, the smaller with fern-draped rocks. The higher rock-pool was a reservoir and its overflow trickled down through drooping ferns to the sand-fringed pool.

A coloured girl had just finished the family washing and was filling the basket with wrung-out clothes. A well-trodden path showed among the trees, probably leading to some coloured people's homes. This was the women's washing-pool.

The girl stood erect with her back to me. With a lithe movement she slipped off her simple dress and stood toying with the soap, admiring her shapely limbs. She had a warm creamy skin delicately tinged with pink. Probably a white girl with a strong dash of Malay. Perhaps a dash of Chinese too, for her hands and feet were delicately small.

I sat with my back to an elm-tree and breathed never a word; it was mean of me, but it was a wonderful picture. How she enjoyed that bath! Pleasure showed in every kittenish action. She smiled as she twisted round to soap her back, sitting quaintly erect to reach the hollow between her shoulder-blades. Then she stood up and let down her hair. It fell like a caressing black shawl right to her knees. With a tortoise-shell comb she combed it, reaching one-half the long tresses over one shoulder, then the rest over the other. When she inclined her head and combed, the hair-tips touched the water. With a single movement she threw the whole black mass over her back. When she sat in the pool the gentle current floated the hair away, leaving one pale shoulder bare. I was eager to see her face. As she stepped from the pool her creamy skin fairly shone.

The lovely stranger mounted the mossy rocks of the little reservoir and gazed at her reflection, stretched, and held up rounded arms, making a seductive little hollow in her back, turned slowly around on the right foot and left toe, smiling over her shoulder at the pool. By Jove, a man's life can hold some glorious moments! My heart thumped at my first perfect thrill.

Suddenly she poised, staring questioningly up at the branches, her cameo little face comically serious. Looking quaintly startled she stared around-sniffing. My tobacco smoke! I froze against the tree as she stared in my direction-her black eyes widened. She screamed, leapt, and flew off down the path as if Satan were at her heels. I laughed and hurried away. Coloured brothers and menfolk see red if suddenly aroused.

I have never forgotten Mee-lele, lovely little animal, warm little human soul. Her eyes would fairly dance to the smile on her lips. She would give all her heart, or else hate passionately. But she liked thrills too much; trouble was the breath of life to her.

Those were happy days on the Bloomfield. Life flowed by as evenly as the beautiful river before us; although that could rise in sullen flood to subside again like the passions of the human beings living upon its banks.

Except when the whole camp was enjoying a thorough loaf, Chulbil and Arthur would be busy in the stockyard breaking in horses, branding, attending to sore backs, or setting the native stockmen to greasing and repairing the long rows of packsaddles and gear. Sometimes they would be twenty miles away in the bush galloping after "scrubbers," or improving the zigzag up which the loaded horses had to scramble to reach the tableland. Norman, Charlie and I would be out pig-hunting, or down the river in the dinghy fishing. More often, each would go about his own business.

One late afternoon, Raleigh came striding down to the Landing from China Camp. He was the tall manager of the Roaring Meg Tin-mining Company, fourteen miles farther south. As always, he was finding life bright and sunny; the world was a gay old dog, and we were hanging to the tail of it. I don't think a man of Raleigh's type could have an enemy in the world. We were glad of the visitor. Only a man coming to or going from "the end of the world" treads that track.

Raleigh had made a little iron non-collapsible canoe. It was his new baby-a beauty. He could pick it up and walk away with it under one arm. And all his own invention. He was going to Cooktown in it.

Not a man of us would have crossed the river in that frail shell; we had *too* much respect for alligators. Raleigh intended to make a thirty-mile sea-trip as well.

"There will be no passengers," laughed Chulbil.

"The fishes will attend to the funeral," joked Charlie.

But Raleigh smiled light-heartedly and next day set off down the river sitting very erect as he paddled the tiny craft on its maiden voyage. The natives watched him rippling along with the down tide. As watermen they were keenly interested but shook their heads over the chances of the "piccaninny canoe."

Several days later natives from miles up the coast helped Raleigh back into the Bloomfield. A breeze had sprung up at sea bringing a broadside wave that capsized the canoe. He straddled it throughout the afternoon and half the night, the tide making him its toy, the sea-gulls shrieking over him, the waves finally bashing him to the shore. The inner sides of his legs were skinned and badly cut where he had been gripping the canoe. It was days before he could walk again. Poor Raleigh, a man of adventures, he went safely through the Great Adventure only to be drowned in a quiet Australian river down south.

The nights were beautiful. Arthur would be lying in his bunk in the big shed, fever-racked or dreaming and planning, the others of us lazing out on the bank high above the water, yarning or listening to the native story-tellers describing adventure, animal hunts, love, or queer mystical things. From the native camp floated the moon-song of the lubras and rhythmic drumming as they clapped hands between their thighs to the stamp of young bucks practising the corroboree. On one such night Charlie slyly said:

"I saw old Assan Rah sharpening his kris to-day."

Norman smiled as he filled his pipe with nigger-twist.

"Who for?" he asked quietly.

"Did he have a look like 'Jack' on his face?" chuckled Chulbil.

I never said a word: it was a silver silence. A night bird swished by and the aboriginals hushed to the sound with superstitious reverence.

"Oh Mee-lele! Mee-lele!" sang Chulbil in his not unpleasant voice, "lil-y of beau-ty, flow'r of the scrub!"

So, someone had been talking!

Mee-lele was Assan's betrothed: he had bought her. She hated him but her father had long ago accepted Assan's money. Someday they were to be married with a great feast; all the river would be invited. Mee-lele with her passionate, youthful longings married to the "Killer of Pigs!" Mee-lele who had been educated at the Convent in distant Thursday Island! Her fresh loveliness, bought by a withered old Malay!

Quite apart from Charlie's mischievous remark I had already been given something to think about in that regard only the night before. When returning along the native track from down-river very late, I had cautiously felt my way down the tree-shadowed bank that leads to the foot-board. This long board crosses the narrow tidal creek that runs in from the river by the Landing wharf, fifty yards down the slope from the shed. This creek is a mud-pond at low tide but at high the board, stretching from bank to bank, is only a foot above water. At high tide, an occasional alligator lurked up this creek on the off chance of grabbing one of the Pierce's dogs. Now and again they snavelled a fowl or two.

So, cautiously I peered down into the black creek before stepping on to the board. On this side of the creek the undergrowth threw shadows as black as the pit. I chanced it, skipped straight across the board and thankfully leapt on to the clear sloping bank opposite. Just ahead, fifty yards away, appeared the dully gleaming roof of the shed. Twenty feet to the right was the riverbank. To the left was the manioc and banana garden adjoining the horse-yard. Farther left still the native camp away in the darkness.

All was well. A man had to be always wary lest any prowling native be about. They are the watchdogs of the river.

A hissing grunt and harsh breaths startled me as feet shuffled forcibly right in front. Men were fighting – and silently! Just the slipping of hands, the grit of teeth as their interlocked forms loomed up wrenching one another down the sloping bank towards the creek. They wrestled, no punching, just gripped the other around the middle, backs arched, chest to chest, deep breaths collapsing in grunts as they strained to throw. Over they thumped and instantly snatched at each other's throat while rolling down the bank. Neither cried out, though a shout would have aroused the dogs and all. I saw as they clawed down the bank that one was Mee-lele's young cousin Ratara, the other was Boongah a flash stockman of the Pierce's, but naked now and back to the fighting stone-age. Across his forehead was painted a sinister red bar. Each struggled to roll the other down there into the blackness of the creek-food for alligators! And neither made a sound except for choking gasps, tearing of grass as knees and feet dug in for leverage.

For a moment they poised right on the brim of the creek thrusting one another in almost a crying madness until the coloured lad throttled the aboriginal over. Quick as an eel he slung his legs around Ratara's neck and both splashed down into the pit.

I never saw two men leave the water with such celerity,

The coloured man sprang to the plank and bounded across into the blackness leading to the settlement while the aboriginal sped into the night towards the camp. It was the grim determination to settle the matter without noise that had been so impressive: a private affair in which they preferred to chance death rather than attract attention. Thinking deeply, I cautiously crept up to my bunk in the shed.

What was Mee-lele's cousin doing up here at this hour so far from the settlement? Had he been spying around our shed, spying on my whereabouts for Assari's information? Perhaps Boongah the stockman had come up to the shed seeking tobacco or orders for the morrow's work, had seen the spy and they had clenched. Hardly that. In such a case the aboriginal would have sneaked away and warned the Pierces, If prevented, he would certainly have yelled. No, it looked a feud, or one of those "private" affairs, over a woman probably.

And I must be silent too.

Norman and Charlie would have listened to the story but have given no true explanation, even though they knew it. My two mates were the best of men but they were blood-brothers of the aboriginals, which has a deeper meaning than white people realize. Native business in any of its hidden aspects was no concern of mine or any other outsider. The Bairds were bound to me in the ordinary ties of mateship, but a deeper tie bound them to honour their native pledge.

Chulbil understood all this. He was in the confidence of the natives, too, but to a considerably lesser degree than the Bairds. He would have listened to everything, then laughed and joked and told nothing. By talking a man might well put his foot into it with those two earnest fighters; be a "big mouth" better closed-by an alligator perhaps.

It was no good inquiring of Arthur. He would have nothing to do with the natives; those that worked for him were paid for it and that was the end of the matter. He would be indignant that the fight had taken place so close to his shed, would order the sullen boy to explain-and then "big mouth" would be right in for it. So I kept the secret. A curious life for a young chap to find himself in, but intensely interesting. And it sharpened his wits considerably.

The first night that I met old Assan, we were all very merry at a coloured person's house. Hammocks were lolled in on the wide veranda, the girls rolling their own cigarettes with deft brown fingers, peeling mango or banana, or taking a noisy hand at cards. Luana was there of course, her irrepressible laughter and witty repartee more than a match for the sly jokes being whispered or called to her along the length of the veranda. Luana was a tireless dancer and a dangerous flirt; she loved to tease men, for which pastime she would probably pay dearly someday. She had a piquant brown face with a quick, winning smile as deceptive as her heart-if she had a heart.

Melissa came hurriedly on to the veranda, smiling a welcome but taking no other notice of Norman, Charlie, or me. Melissa was a nice girl, on the quiet side, with large brown eyes and hair of microscopic curls. She busied herself with the cards and would not look where her heart lay.

The coloured men ranged from very dark to the lightest brown, the majority of them slimly-built, agile fellows; expert swimmers among the coral reefs, and sailor lads all. Good lookers among them too. Their clean-cut features, coal-black hair, brown eyes, and white teeth helped them a lot. They appeared very cool in clean white singlet, khaki pants, and belt. All were barefooted.

The girls were in light, flimsy dress, generally displaying brown or creamy legs, but as a rule large feet for they seldom wore shoes. They were proud of their hair which was as diversified as their colour shades. A variegated croton leaf or gaily coloured flower would attract a man's attention to their hair, then to their face. The eyes would do the rest.

Piles of papaws, sour-sops, and bananas were on the table, while now and again a resounding bang on the iron roof told that flying-foxes were playing havoc among the golden mangoes in the trees. Hurricane lamps swung along the veranda.

Bright eyes flashed a challenge to eyes that instantly answered. Jealousy lay hidden under many a light word and laugh, or scowled openly on brow and gleaming teeth. But only one who understood them would have sensed the undercurrents of feeling that pulsed through these people's ever ready hospitality.

At midnight Assan, wizened and small, appeared on the veranda, mud and grass-fluff glued between his toes, a rifle in one hand and half a pig, dripping blood, slung over his shoulder. His khaki shorts showed stumpy brown legs muscled like an animal's. His crinkled yellow-brown face smiled at everyone as he peered from small, bright brown eyes that did not smile with his face. A green-eyed, spotted dog stood at his side. Assan would have killed any man who dared to touch that dog. But so would any man in that country who hurt his pig-dog.

We greeted Assan noisily; not because this was his house, but because he was the Killer of Pigs. His jungle craft supplied the meat for a number of coloured homes when they were out of beef or tinned stuff. He was a man of understandable value. Whole families would have gone meat hungry many a time but for him.

Any man can go pig-shooting; but the man is rare indeed who can go after a pig and invariably make a kill. Assan was such a man. He would never give up. Across the grass-entangled plain to the big scrub mountains miles back he would travel with a crouching swiftness and disappear into the scrub like a shadow. He never wore boots. He understood the ways of the wild pig better than most men know their children. With a merciless persistence he would hunt along those rock-bound gorges and up those gloomy ravines in silent company with his green-eyed dog.

There is danger in hunting the wild pig in his own mountain fastnesses. He is the true wild pig, the descendant of those liberated by Captain Cook on the Endeavour River over a hundred years ago. In his reversion he has grown prodigiously, occasional boars have been weighed at four hundred-weight. The snout has lengthened considerably and the shoulders have grown notoriously powerful. The hide on neck and shoulders is a quarter of an inch thick, sometimes more. A bullet must strike them between the eyes, directly behind the ear, or directly behind the shoulder to bring them straight down. When wounded a boar will charge the first moving thing he sees, and he comes at a speed that puts the wind well up a man. In the big scrubs, I have never met a man who, hunting without a well-trained pigdog, did not look around for a handy tree before firing at a boar. The vines give a man no chance should the pig charge. Roots and canes trip him up, whereas the swine comes straight through.

The lower tusks of a boar are cruel ivories – up to eight inches long on a big old boar – razor-edged where, as a rule, they circle round and wear against the smaller ones of the upper jaw.

A charging boar can rip open a horse if he only gets the thrust at the right angle. Norman one day found a boar's skull, the tusks of which had missed contact with those of the upper teeth, and, ultimately, had pierced the skull.

The wild pig of those mountains is a very different proposition to the station pig gone wild down south.

A Queensland Tantanoola Tiger.

8

THE SCRUBBERS

By way of variety we gave the Pierces a hand to run in scrubbers. Scrubbers are wild cattle that venture out into the forest edge to feed, generally at night but not always, returning to the sheltering scrubs at the first alarm. The Pierces were starting a "run," had taken up a block of country and stocked it with a few head. As opportunity occurred between the visits of the supply-boat, they would reclaim a few wild cattle from the distant ranges.

So leaving Arthur to mind the Landing we rode away, our horses lively, Chulbil and Charlie singing as usual when together, stock-boys yelling back farewells to the native camp, Norman and I riding soberly behind, happy as Larry. The smoke from our pipes coiled straight up in the glorious air; the laden packhorses moved along impishly, prick-eared, slyly seeking a chance for a kick at the wary dogs. Leaning well forward in the saddle as the horses scrambled up the zigzag, Chulbil was alternately yelling jokes in lingo to the blackboys high up ahead, or shouting to the rogues when those cunning beasts twisted round and stood, purposely blocking the path. From the tableland we left the beaten track and went bush straight west, crossing the Meg and riding out into "No Man's" country. There are no such things as fences on those grassy flats intersected by innumerable steep-banked ravines and bounded by ridges and hills. It is fascinating to see the country spread out far away below you like a living map, well grassed, and timbered with a wonderful variety of trees. It was a bonny day. A pheasant called hoarsely from the blady grass, to be answered by its mate clinging to a box-tree sapling as she swayed her long tail. A drongo in glossy black coat and metallic green wings cackled loudly as we rode by, then hurriedly changed his tune to an imitation of a noisy starling. A crowd of yellow-breasted figbirds passed the time of the day in a loud, disputing manner of voice. From a lilac tree a hefty black butcher-bird regarded us aggressively, his head cocked sideways, his hooked bill cruelly suggestive. Chulbil shouted and pointed the bird out as he rode on ahead.

"Come and see the butcher's shop," invited Norman and turned his horse towards the tree.

It was a needlewood-tree, armed with inch-long spikes. Dead and dying fruit not of the tree were impaled on those spikes. Small lizards, large beetles, wriggling grubs, drooping mice, and several gay butterflies (their wings still palpitating) spoke dumbly of the butcher-bird's energy in stocking his meat-safe. His friends, jealous of the common hoard, harshly ordered us away.

Just at sunset the neddies pushed through the grass on to a broad scrub creek. Farther in among those big trees was a calm pool like a miniature lake with its little sandy beach. We slung the packs on the sand and hobbled the impatient neddies who immediately plunged through the trees back to the forest and grass.

Some months beforehand, Chulbil and his blackboys had built a yard here in the virgin bush, some three miles from our present camp. The yard was in a strategic position on a grassy flat, a favourite feeding-ground of the scrubbers. Running out from the yard were two wings of rough bush .fencing. These wings formed a bottle-neck or "brake" which led to the trapping-yard. Once get the cattle to the mouth of that brake and it only meant a rushing gallop to start them along it and right into the yard.

The cattle would come from the scrubs lining the mountain tops and sides then mooch down among the trees of the creek and emerge on to the open forest upon the hillslopes where the good grass was. Some time ago, the Pierces had driven "coachers" out on to this particular feeding-ground and left them there.

Coachers are cattle trained to help trap their wild brethren. They are cunning old stagers, never flurried, never excited; they represent the acme of confidence beasts among cattle. Their job is to get by degrees into the confidence of the wild chaps who poke out from the scrub; then as the days go by to lure them farther and farther out on to the feeding-grounds, towards the stockyard, to familiarize them with it until the real day comes. Then in the heat of the fear and excitement they suddenly take the lead and land their trusting brethren right inside.

Wild cattle are often companionable, and curious at the sight of strange cattle. Invariably, after a time, they will come out, mix with the strangers, and then feed with them. The scrubber at first tries to lure the coacher into the scrub only to find himself when too late a prisoner to his fellow's treachery and man's guile. Chulbil had set his trap craftily for the scrubbers that patronized this particular scrub creek. After dawn next morning, we rode quietly up the opposite side of the creek, the heavy wall of trees between us and the feeding-ground. Luckily there was no wind to betray us to the cattle's keen sense of smell. We halted when opposite where we judged the yard to be. Chulbil and a blackboy dismounted and walked in through the creek to return elated a few minutes later.

"There's a dozen of 'em," laughed Chulbil with his eyes rolling. "The coachers are just heading them out towards the yard. Now don't show yourselves until I ride out!"

Charlie laughed and wheeled his horse, sitting the animal as if part of it.

We separated and spread up and down the creek, then, dismounting, led our horses wherever practicable through the trees and into the creek. I crossed at a rocky place where fallen logs lay moss green; but the rough bank oppo, site was shelving and the horse bounded up easily. Through the trees the cattle were visible quietly feeding out on the open forest and some distance down a gentle slope. The mouth of the "brake" leading to the yard. was in full view. The old coachers were feeding out in the lead, gradually drawing in towards the far-flung wings of the brake.

The old horse sniffed what was doing although he was well back among the trees. He held his head high, his ears pricked and twitching.

Time passed. The little mob feeding there in the sunlight drew nearer and nearer the brake. Then came a pause in the feeding, when odd beasts are liable to drift aside with thoughts of a lie down in the shade. Chulbil suddenly rode out into the forest and reined in, two cattle-dogs prick-eared at his horse's heels.

Quickly we rode out in line, well apart, the blackboys on the flanks, their eager dogs in soft-voiced leash. We moved forward quietly; the mob down below were standing now.

We got well towards them before one of the beasts turned his head. He stared and wheeled around, sniffing the air. In a moment other beasts were staring; most wheeled around but the coachers moved quietly off towards the brake. Hesitantly, with an uneasy glance behind, several of the wild cattle followed them; others watched in nervous alarm this line of horsemen advancing between them and the scrub. We moved faster, all keyed up, holding our horses in check. The rustling grass smelled fresh and sweet.

A baldy scrubber swung his neck from side to side then broke, loping swiftly out towards the right flank. With a yell we were in full gallop, the blackboys racing on the flanks, the dogs going like blue streaks to turn four breakaways. The coachers moved soberly until with frightened beasts on their heels they broke into a jogging canter for the brake. To a thunder of hooves, yells, and cracking of whips the blackboys on the right swept down on the breakaways, the dogs leaping at their noses, swerving them until, seeing their mates hurrying below and thinking them escaping, they galloped with flying tails to rejoin them. The mob was now going pell-mell towards the wings and entered them as we galloped down with a wild yelling and volleying of whips as the lane narrowed and the frantic beasts plunged into the yard. It had been a capture at the gallop, as fast as it was easy.

Several hours later the coachers were liberated.

The captives must stay several days. When hunger and thirst overcame their fear of humans, they would be allowed out for a short hungry feed with the coachers, herded by men and dogs, and eventually as they tamed would be driven many miles away and mixed with tame cattle.

Meanwhile, scattered in twos over many miles, we rode from daylight until dark. The plan of campaign now was to disturb, but with caution, what scrubbers we could from the creeks and scrub edges, to scare them away by our presence but always towards the creek we had first operated on. Then on the last day we would round up the country surrounding this creek.

9

LIFE OF THE WILDS

My riding companion was Toby, a native with a cheerful countenance who privately thought me a fool worth fleecing. So, on the promise of payment of "Capistan" tobacco when the stores arrived from Cooktown, with energetic goodwill he neglected his master's work and became my natural history instructor. Nigger-twist, you must know, is native's tobacco, but "Capistan" is "white man tobacco." Among those tangled granite hills and tea-tree swamps and quiet lonely creeks he showed me the queerest of plants; plants that live on the blood of living things as well as on air and soil, plants that live on other plants, plants that live only under stones or wedged in the deep crevices of rocks, plants that draw their sustenance from the decomposition of rotted wood. He even showed me plants that squeak when you press them in a certain way, that shoot out a venomous little puff of powder, that grip with claws, and with sticky stuff, and with spikes, and by suction; plants that do undreamed of things and live in undreamed of ways. And as he showed me so he talked, the whites of his eyes gleaming when he laughed to the flash of perfect teeth that could crunch bone. He had that common urge in the young native anxious to break away from the tribal laws and rule of the old men. He was a "civilized" boy. He answered cheerfully to "Toby," but sulked all day if one called him by his native name. And he must always be spoken to in "English," in which language he answered.

"This plurry plant no plurry good," he said one day in quite angry tones, "him plurry liar, dirty murderer, eat him altogether wild bee!"

The aboriginal's greatest delicacy is wild honey.

The plant he condemned was fastened to a tree trunk. From between its apparently painted small brown-green leaves grew small vase-shaped snow-white flowers with an inviting scent. In each tiny cup lay a diamond of honey dew; and on a drooping stem hung two dainty knobs like russet-brown peas. With an expression of extreme dislike Toby jerked off and opened one of these peas and revealed a rounded white pearl. It was really a shroud of petals holding tight the remains of a native bee. After the flower has sucked the life-blood from its prey it slowly opens its petals and ejects the husk, to await in deathly beauty its next victim.

The natives dislike the bee-eater for the same reason.

Toby showed me many other things – a lot I already knew. But I never let him know *that*. I just inquired of everything in surprised and childlike innocence. A native becomes annoyed if he thinks he is telling you something "big" only to find out that you know all about it.

He showed me one day the rudiments of animal reasoning. Call it what you will, I have been long convinced that animals have more horse-sense than we give them credit for. Riding along the edge of a scrub creek we heard a splashing.

"Piggy-Piggy," chuckled Toby, "catch him pish!"

We slipped off the horses and crawled through the timber. In a small pool about a foot deep a wild pig was splashing methodically back and forth, stirring up the mud and black, decaying leaves. A shimmer of leaping silver in the fast muddying water betrayed the agitation of fish. When the pool was well stirred the pig started walking to and fro across the deeper end, gradually approaching a tiny shingled beach at the shallow end. Agitated flurries on the surface showed where the fish were being driven into the shallow. One leapt clear of the water and landed on the shingle, kicking gaspingly. The fisherman shoved his snout in the water, rooting and thrusting from side to side as he advanced. Suddenly he plunged forward then jerked up holding fast a fish. He gurgled throatily as he gulped it. Grunting hastily he plunged his snout in again, working the faster at this taste of the meal. At the shingle edge he was gobbling, gurgling, and grunting as the blinded fish floundered against his legs and snout.

Natives often secure fish in a similar way, but the pig fisherman excited my interest. I have since watched them fishing, with their snout deep down in the pure mud, for the fish that bury themselves there awaiting the rain. I have watched the beggars nosing for shell-fish and crabs in the pools among the mangrove roots, and seen them in straight out fights with the big savage barramundi that cruise in the water-grass swamps farther up north in the Peninsula.

One late afternoon before the final muster, Toby and I were riding towards camp when a wild yell rang through the trees. There was Chulbil racing down a hillslope, a red beast all out before him. There was no chance of turning the maddened thing before it would reach the shelter of a scrub, but Chulbil, racing by its withers, leaned over and sent the beast flying on its nose. As his horse propped, Chulbil leapt straight off on to the beast, and before the partly-stunned thing could rise had tied its foreleg to its hind-hoof. The marvellous horsemanship, the timing, the throw, the tying were the work of seconds. We galloped up whooping as Chulbil wiped the sweat from his brow. The beast was bellowing and kicking upon the flattened grass, securely "handcuffed." He would stay so until coachers could be driven up, when, huddled amongst them, his head lowered in terrified submission, he would be driven to join his mates who had already tasted man's dominion.

There is nerve and knack in that throwing of a beast at the full gallop. It is a twitch of the tail that does it. A beast can be thrown in a complete somersault-if the man and horse know how!

The concluding day of our little round-up was hell for leather from the word. go. And Chulbil nearly broke his neck at sundown.

Each man had his separate job in the team, the idea being to eventually drive all beasts together and down on to the coachers. Two hours after sunrise, yells and distant whip-cracking told that the fun had started. My horse plunged forward, as eager as I. He knew his job!

Down the forest spur two scrubbers were standing, alarmed at the hoarse bellowing and the ringing crack of whips. I leaned forward in the saddle and away we went. So did the scrubbers – straight back past me, to crash into the scrub. They were gone. So was I, nearly – over the horse's head. I could feel the very disgust in his panting, see it in his eye as his nostrils quivered towards the scrub. Well, it was not for me to go racing clown into the low country with two scrubbers rollicking ahead and I fancy the crowd did not expect it either. So away again we raced towards the nearest cracking whip.

That was a mad ride, down hills, over gullies, plunging up banks, the wind singing past a man's face, his hat whipped off in the timber, a gasp and clenching of the knees as the horse grazed a leaning tree. Hanging on, with his heart in his mouth as logs showed momentarily amongst the grass-a breathless exhilaration all through the racing danger. A pheasant squawked from the horse's hooves as we leapt a gully almost on top of a wallaby. We flew down a ridge and joined Charlie who was riding like a madman, equalled by the streak that was his dog. The thing seemed flying as it leaped logs to vanish in grass and reappear racing to the flank as Charlie's scrubbers swerved. We kept them going so fast they couldn't wheel away. We got a glimpse of Norman and a blackboy racing down a side spur and I marvelled how the horses kept their feet. Wheeling through a line of trees we saw the coachers feeding away down on the flat, and the scrubbers lumbered towards them seeking sanctuary with kind. All hands converged to a thunder of hooves, yells, and crack of whips as the pairs of men came tearing down with or without their catches. I laughed on seeing I was not the only one who had lost. As the scattered beasts ran into the coachers they set off on the run for the distant yards. We followed on the rear and flanks and with a wild whoop set off after the breakaways. A few got away, for we had to keep the mob on the run.

It was right at the entrance to the wings that Chulbil came to grief. A big red steer with nasty horns swerved out from the mob and raced back; Chulbil whooped and galloped straight at him, but the steer came the. faster with lowered head, mad eyes, and slavering mouth. Chulbil's horse made its one last mistake and the horns impaled its chest to a horrible grunting impact. The horse crashed straight over the beast which thumped back on its haunches to collapse forward on its knees then rise groggily. Chulbil went flying many yards, and we thought his neck was broken. It wasn't, but that night he was nearly crying over the loss of his favourite horse.

Chulbil and his blackboys were to stay by the cattle until such time as the scrubbers were sufficiently tamed to be driven away with the coachers. Norman and Charlie and I rode away back to the Bloomfield.

10

MEE-LELE

SEVERAL families of the coloured people were going picnicking for a few days out to the Hope Islands. Two coloured boys rowed up-river bearing an invitation with a special request for" Jacky."

"Right up in Society," laughed Chulbil, who had just returned from the mustering-camp. "They want our Jack to give tone."

"Give a bag of flour more likely," grimaced Charlie, "when the stores come."

"Assan wants him under his eye," smiled Norman soberly, "he's safer there." Charlie was oiling the rifle. He drew the pull-through through the barrel, held his thumbnail at the breech, and squinted down at the bright grooves inside.

"Look out there's not an accident, Jack," he said with his eye glued to the muzzle, "Assan knows that none of us others are going."

They didn't either; they had other business on hand. So I was the one white man sailing with a happy-go-lucky crowd down the river. We went in Assan's cutter, a little five-ton, smelly, *bêche-de-mer* vessel in which he had made cruises worthy of a Viking. He stood at the tiller now, his little bright eyes puckered up as he gazed seaward, smiling his mirthless smile. Assan was a wonderful sailor; the blood of the sea was born in him. Though the coloured people were wary of him, somehow or other I liked Assan. It may have been the generosity of youth, or the feeling that all life was grand and a wonderful adventure, but the grim old chap inspired a friendly feeling.

As the cutter's bows rose to the open sea the sails bellied and the vessel skimmed along to a hiss of spray. With a twitch of his wrist on the tiller Assan dipped the bowsprit under and chuckled to the shrieks as the girls took the shower-bath. The sea was a turquoise blue, the waves lazily rolling in, the water sparkling under the sunlight that bathed the thickly wooded shores astern. Everyone was happy; the girls were out for the time of their lives, while the young men rolled cigarettes and joked to sallies that brought peals of laughter. Nearly naked youngsters crawled about the packed vessel like ants. Young Ratara was there, looking spick and span in his white singlet and khaki trousers, his coal-black hair bare to the sun, his clear-cut face smiling as if he had never a care in the world.

The islands soon showed up, dull green, with shining patches of sand here and there. They are only twelve miles from the river-mouth, and a lively sou'-easter blew us there in no time. Both islands, one of coral, the other mainly sand, are very low-lying and covered with mangroves and dwarf shrubbery. A huge coral-reef spreads under and around them. When the tide is out you can, in places, walk over it for a mile "out to sea."

As we sailed in over the reef hosts of terns and silver gulls greeted us in shrieking clouds, the swish from their wings fanning us as one racing cloud swooped low over the mast. At the coral edge and on the beaches, cranes and herons, white, black, grey, and brown, regarded us non-committally.

A mob of solemn pelicans swam up quite close to the cutter, giving us the once over before carrying on with their fishing. They folded enormous beaks down upon their breasts and watched in severe meditation while we dropped the anchor. A frigate-bird and a dozen white-bellied sea-eagles circled above, waiting to pirate fish from their weaker brethren. From the trees came the boo-hoo-hoo! of the Torres Strait pigeon. Eagerly the girls pointed out the birds, like big White flowers among the foliage. All were in laughing haste to land, but Assan would not allow a man overside until the sails were furled shipshape.

We rowed the camp gear ashore to a bustling and chattering. A sham upsetting of the crowded dinghies by the men was followed on shore by dignified argument and much laughing over the choosing of the women's quarters.

In late afternoon the pigeons began to come home, first in swift flying scores, then in flocks, later in unceasing clouds until the branches of the trees were swaying as if under a heavy wind. We could hardly talk above the boo-hoo-hooing, the fighting and squabbling of the birds. It was sheer slaughter shooting into them but we had many hungry mouths to feed as evidenced by a dozen cooking-fires.

Those were merry nights, but noisy; noisy from our own laughing, joking, singing crowd, and infernally noisy from the birds. They would sleep for a couple of hours then break out into a violent quarrelling and flustering among the branches, whether disturbing one another out of pure cussedness or because of prowling nocturnal things I don't know. Both, the coloured people said.

We would hardly settle to sleep again when a shriek from the women's quarters would alarm everyone but Assan. No fear of Assan leaving his blanket just because a crab or water-rat had nibbled a girl's leg.

We spent the days exploring shady recesses among the shrubbery, collecting birds' eggs, walking out on the reef at low tide, fishing, swimming, and lazing. The girls had brought scanty but pleasing bathing dresses of their own make which they delighted to show off as much as they did to swim and dive.

The reef at low tide was as fascinating as the jungle. It was a sea jungle alive with multitudinous forms of life: fish, animal, vegetable; half-fish and half-vegetable, ranging from microscopic to gigantic. At times one couldn't distinguish where the vegetable ended and the fish or animal began. The live corals were often as beautiful and variegated as the lovely parrot-fish that swam amongst them. Numbers of the coral fish were red, brown, or green, and these swam only in those pools enclosed by like-coloured coral.

"Look at the baby fishes, Jacky," called Mee-lele one afternoon. "They're really grown-ups, and they've stolen the rainbow for dresses."

In a pool that was a sea garden swam a number of fishes not an inch long. Lively little beggars in brilliant colours, they swam up to us inquisitively. Mee-lele threw a coral into the water and laughed gaily as they disappeared into a huge sea-cabbage. Its leaves closed protectingly around them and the pool remained crystal clear with not a fish in it. A few minutes later the queer leaves of the giant cabbage began slowly to unfold. Presently the leader glided out very alertly and halted an inch from the cabbage, his tiny head turned ready to dart back into sanctuary, his wee tail just keeping him as if poised in crystal. Another jerked out beside him followed by others until soon all were cruising swiftly around the pool.

"Come and I'll show you something big now," laughed Mee-lele eagerly as she led me away. "Oh I hate those things; they give me the creeps." And she grimaced at a squashed-out, black, rubbery-like thing that pulsed with life under her feet. We peered into a circular pool covering another sea garden. Deep down in that garden, camouflaged by waving tresses of mermaid's hair, gaped a huge oval thing revealing uncanny flesh colours of red, green, and purple.

"You see what it is!" pointed Mee-lele.

"Yes. A giant clam."

"Oh! You know all about it."

"No, I don't Mee-lele. I only guessed it from the little ones that squirt up water on the reef."

"Well, I'll show you something about them you don't know!" And she dived straight down, the loveliest little thing that ever entered that garden pool.

Uneasily I stared down at those pale, kicking heels. The giant clams of the Great Barrier Reef can be dangerous under certain circumstances. Divers are always wary of them. The little fool closed that giant shell. She punched her arm straight into the wide open flesh and withdrew it on the instant. As the great mouth shut she sped up smiling through water to laugh on the surface and splash my frown away.

"You look quite nice when angry, Jacky. Smile or I'll do it again when he opens."

"You may never smile again if you do, Mee-lele. If that thing closed on your arm I couldn't help you. You would be drowned long before we could bring a bar and tomahawks to chop it open."

"Cautious Jacky! Always thinking of what *might* happen. Come on over to the edge of the reef and I'll show you the sharks. I love them. So creepy and cruel and swift. Just like Assan – especially when he smiles."

"Now look here, Mee-lele," I protested as we walked out to the reef edge, "old Assan is not half a bad chap if you take him right."

She laughed and pointed out to where a swarm of triangular fins were cleaving the water as sharks drove a shoal of fish close against the reef. When the frantic fish were packed tight the sharks sped amongst them biting their prey in halves, hissing through the water in tigerish attacks.

"You see," the girl said as we watched the slaughter, "the sharks get them just where they want them and then – but come over here, Jacky, I'll show you Assan's smile."

"Assan's what?"

"Assan's smile! I'll show you the eye of a tiger shark! "

"Oh I say, Mee-lele, let the old chap off lighter than that!"

She turned on me, her face pale and tremulous with fury.

"You haven't got to live with him," she hissed.

"If ever I have *to,* I'll make him wish he was never born!"

I did not argue. After all, it was the girl's own life she was crying about. Assan had had his day, but she was never to have a chance. She stared with parted lips while the colour slowly drained back into her face.

"Oh Jacky," she smiled in swift remorse, "I'm the most horrid girl in the world and I want you to think me wonderful."

She kissed me quite regardless of others who might be *out* on *the* reef or lazing among *the* trees.

"Forgive me, Jacky. You white men do not understand. Why should I have to marry a man I hate when I want life and love and happiness? You do not understand how cruel are the customs of my people."

This was the bird season, a time of hysterical energy, of intense concentration, of sublime achievement in the bird-world. Eggs were everywhere. Sometimes we walked on them; we could not help it. The pigeons built bulky homes of green twigs in a slapdash style, and told the whole world about it. Other tree birds, not liking the company, had to take the smaller shrubs and pandanus-palms. Smaller birds, the regular habitues of the island, made cunning, well-concealed homes, sometimes little swinging ones hidden among the thick drooping leaves of the palms. The sea-birds laid their big spotted eggs wherever the surroundings were so like the colour of the eggs as to make them almost invisible. Rats, crabs, and pirate birds grew overbearing and fat during the egg season. In fact the island life profited directly or indirectly by the egg harvest. We did well too.

These people were adepts at choosing bait for the different kinds of fish. They knew the shellfish, the sea-shore things, and numerous hard-to-get-at growths for which the fish foraged all day among the reefs. Above all they knew the delicacies for which the fish often long in vain. Should a shoal of fastidious fish refuse ordinary bait, these men knew just where to seek some particular sea-growth and how to cut down to its heart for the luxury for which particular fish would fight like sharks.

I liked to hear old Assan talk in the evenings. The reflections from our big fire playing on the water's edge, the island dark behind us, the pigeons shuffling among the trees, a crab or water-rat rustling among the loose coral, tuned us listeners to Assan's tales of the jungle or the sea or weird spirit beings. Some of his vampire stories put Dracula's among simple ghost stories. The girls used to listen breathlessly, their big brown eyes shining in the firelight. Little wonder that the scamper of a rat over bare feet caused shrieks at night.

These are only tiny islands, but they contain a world of interest. I was sorry when the order came -"All aboard the cutter."

We were taking some hundreds of half-cooked pigeons and smoke-dried fish back with us to the folks at home.

Old Assan had to shout out threats of "the tide!" before the last noisy dinghy-load was brought aboard. As the boys trooped forward to haul up the anchor Mee-lele touched my arm and pointed overside. There swam a tiger shark, several fathoms under water, effortlessly circling the lugger. It was rather a creepy feeling watching that lithe grey shape down there, knowing that he was watching us. Assan slipped quietly down to the tiny cabin for his rifle on the off chance that the menace might come to the surface.

"Dive down, Mee-lele," laughed Luana, "and give Assan a shot at him."

"You think I'm frightened," answered Mee-lele scornfully.

"I'm sure!"

Mee-lele turned to me with the prettiest little smile.

"Neither shark will get me, Jack!" and she dived over.

Straight down too, turned round under water and sped up for the cutter.

Without the flicker of an eyelid Assan levelled his rifle. I prayed with all my heart he would get just one chance to shoot. The shark wheeled and sped straight for the girl. Smiling up at us she broke the surface with the shark at her heels as we snatched her arms. I saw his teeth but with the crack of the rifle he snapped them shut and vanished.

The girl, panting on the deck, laughed up at us.

"I told you, Jacky – the shark would not get me!"

"It will be a good shark that takes Mee-lele, Jack," smiled Assan from eyes that did not smile.

I just gazed at that fool girl. There was nothing to reply, anyway. But how I admired Assan! The nerve, the coolness while he calculated his shot to the last second, until the shark was so close that the concussion must take effect. And at that precise instant it was right on the girl.

An alligator caught at Halifax, Queensland 1920.

11

THE DANCE

WE tried hard to kill Big-nose. We sought him from the sheltering scrub that lines the high banks; we hid among the tall grasses where forest borders the winding bends; we lay in wait along the mangrove-shrouded banks of the lower river; and in the bottom of a canoe drifting downstream with the tide, like a log, as the alligator himself loved to drift.

But Big-nose possessed the cunning of the Evil One; he evaded our craftiest plans as if forewarned. The coloured people say that when once an alligator has eaten a man he is possessed of an evil spirit which warns him of human vengeance.

We sewed strychnine inside the carcass of a goat and set it floating down the stream. Three days later, the tide washed a poisoned alligator up on the beach down at the river-mouth. But it was not Big-nose.

"I'll show you how to kill alligators, Jack," smiled Antonio's big son one morning. So we rowed downstream and borrowed a nanny-goat with a young kid. In a likely spot, under the mangroves that shaded a gloomy creek, we securely tied the goat and then hid ourselves among the logs and grass overlooking those mud-slimed roots below. Evening came settling down quiet and still, the shadows deepened, the tree-leaves whispered with the night, and the tide came creeping in, creeping up towards the goat. A bittern boomed hollowly. We listened to suckings and whisperings as the water gurgled over mud and sand and roots. A flying-fox shrieked. The goat stared around in sniffing alarm, her eyes big and glassy. She tugged at her lashing, and bleated distressfully as she tried to break away towards us. She was pathetically anxious and afraid; she was heavy with milk too. We unmuzzled the kid but held it while it awakened the creek with its bleatings. Loudly the mother cried to join it, tugging at the rope, calling to the kid with all a mother's fervour.

Young Antonio grasped my wrist while staring through the grass. Coming on the dark water just behind the goat were two shadowy nuts, with larger, harder ones behind them. Without the faintest sound the alligator's snout rose clear of the water, then his horny back as he waddled ashore, Satan's cunning in the crouch of his long body as he crept up to grab.

A man experiences a deep joy in aiming at an alligator, especially when the treacherous reptile is creeping up on something. It is a wonderful thrill to level a rifle right between those horrid eyes.

On three different nights we got an alligator with the aid of the same goat. But it ended in tragedy. On the last night our prey did not come until very late and dark, then he crawled up the bank so cautiously that it was hard to distinguish his loathsome bulk from the mud. Then, as the rifle-flash illuminated trees, reptile, and goat there was a sudden rush, something snapped, something plunged into the water. I could have cried in intense self-disgust, thinking that the alligator had escaped until we heard its tail lashing in its own death struggles.

But the other alligator had got away with the goat. Going home, the kid bleated pitifully all the way. We felt like murderers!

We continued seeking Big-nose, and opposite the Landing, at the dangerous hole by the ford where the horsemen cross over, we set a chain to a "springy" tree, craftily baiting a smellful lump of meat around a huge iron hook, and tied a bullock-bell to the branch by the top end of the chain. What an outrageous clattering that bell made, clanging up the river like a fire-engine gone mad! We leaped from bunks and grabbed hurricane lamps as yelling natives came running from the camp. Snatching up rifles, we raced down to the Landing and tumbled into dinghies with native rowers already at the oars. Then a race across the pitch-black river, the unseen tide hissing and slapping the dinghy and that mad bell clanging in furious jerks. We landed downstream, for with the lanterns held aloft we could glimpse the chain ripping backwards and forwards and jerking outstream. It would have cut a dinghy in two. It slackened as we climbed up the bank, for the beast could sense, hear, or see the dinghies; but we could not see it, peer as we might. Chulbil yelled to the natives to pull back for gelignite and a piece of fencing-wire. We would take no chance of our prey escaping during the hours before dawn.

When the dinghies came racing back, Chulbil made a loop of the wire around the chain. "I wonder how old Big-nose will like his necklace," he laughed as he fastened six plugs of gelignite around the wire. We lit the fuse and the wire skidded down the chain. A couple of feet below the water pearly bubbles arose from the fuse, where the wire had caught on the slack. All hands grabbed the chain and tugged. Instantly it was jerked from our hands while the vibration sent the wire loop straight down to the alligator. We struck the chain with a sapling to keep him jerking and thus bring the loop right to his snout, over it probably. The explosion came in a heavy rumble, sending up a waterspout that smacked back upon the river to a harsh clang of the bell. Hissing wavelets slapped the bank under us.

In the morning we pulled a sixteen-footer from the river. But he was not Big-nose.

A native canoed up from the island tribe downstream to tell of Big-nose tracks in the mangrove mud on the seaward side of the river. So we made a day of it in a native canoe. All we got was a feed of turtle's eggs, an interesting day, and an alligator's nest. That was among the mangrove at the sea entrance just above tide-mark, a mound of sand, mangrove leaves, grass, and quite a lot of mussel shells: she had scraped them from a heap where travelling natives had roasted the fish. Six inches deep in the nest were fifty long, dirty white eggs, considerably larger than hens' eggs. The natives grabbed them eagerly, while we were pleased. I t meant that fifty alligators would never be born.

For all that, don't imagine that alligators are plentiful in our northern rivers. They are not. Each river has its few "old men," each one claiming a portion of the river for himself. The nastiest of these give the river its reputation. You might row up a river for half a day and only see one alligator. There are more of course. The farther north you go, the more plentiful they become-or appear.

As a rule, they are found more in the wide stretches of mangrove swamps fringing the majority of river-mouths, than in the river itself. They breed there too. The vicious youngsters can look after themselves practically from the moment they bite through their shells. They scuttle off into the sheltering mangrove roots lest the old man come waddling along and eat them.

For all their treacherous ways, their strength and cunning, very rarely a human gets caught. Because, I suppose, the wary human so rarely gives them a chance.

The settlement was in a hubbub; Antonio was giving a dance. Busy preparations were being made. The great night was to be one week from today. A dinghy came upstream and one of Antonio's own sons stepped ashore and gave us a smiling invitation.

It was a moonlit night. The mangroves lining the northern bank threw a wall of black shadow on the silvered stream. The sky was a glorious velvet pinpricked with a million stars. The rowlocks clicked musically as Norman pulled and sang. Chulbil sat in the stern, alternately singing and blowing a mouth-organ, Charlie played the concertina and sang, while I looked up wondering at the beauty of the sky and mountain shadows. From down-river the blare of conch shells came hoarsely to us, intermingled with the boom of wooden drums. When passing the big island we saw drummers silhouetted by the flames. They were a circle of squatting lubras drumming their thighs, singing in rising and falling voices to barbaric rhythm. Harshly, but with a wild melody that filled the river, there came the savage song of men, the stamp of feet, the clash of shields as they danced in honour of Antonio's dance. Farther downstream lights ferried across the stream as guests sang their way to the dance. At Antonio's lanterns hung from the veranda on the hill and from the doorway a broad splash of light shone across the garden and out on to the river. On the path leading up the slope we could see white-clad figures flitting among the banana groves. They turned and yodelled to us as Chulbil arose and bawled a native war-song. His effort was rewarded by a series of war yells from over the water and up on the hill. We pulled up at Antonio's "wharf" to a defiant bray of conches.

On the veranda Antonio welcomed us with a grave courtesy. A tall, swarthy Portuguese, with piercing black eyes, he was a stern-faced man. Much travelled, he could, when in the mood to talk, hold us enthralled. He was a type of the old Portuguese sea-rover, every inch a man, but ruthless and hard. Although he could always get the natives to work for him, they feared him more than they did any "white" man. Antonio courteously waved us into the Big Room, then turned to greet other guests.

Huge shields grotesquely carved and painted in bright ochres; head-dresses of parrot, crane, and bird-of-paradise plumes; forehead bands picked out with pearl-shell and cat's-eyes, spears, bows and arrows, clubs and wommeras, doads, wooden swords, human-bone and cassowary-skin daggers; native skirts in dyed grasses; sun-baked and stuffed human heads, and other things covered the walls of the big room.

The men were in shirt-sleeves, smiling faced, smoking as they talked of trochus and the sea, of pearl and *bêche-de-mer*, of gardens and luggers and family affairs.

The quaintly dressed girls were plainly out for a night of it, judging by the laughter coming from the chattering groups and from the dressing-room. Those girls were good looking, three of them lovely. Mee-lele especially so as she glided straight towards me, smiling in shy defiance.

What a wild, gay dance that was, as were nearly all our Bloomfield dances. Everyone laughing, the music lively and willing, fiddles and concertinas going their hardest, the serious-faced orchestra putting their soul into it, their foreheads, bare brown necks and chests soon gleaming with sweat. How the boards thumped while the flying-foxes squealed outside! How the crowd chattered and danced and laughed and miraculously caught every word. Old-time dances, waltz, schottische, and quaint old Spanish movements to a lilting music and dreamy, swaying step.

Trying to dodge the wiles of Mee-lele I became aware of something serious going on in an inner room. I shouldered my way in. A knot of older men were gathered round a couch over which one held a lantern. Their deep-lined faces were set and grim. A coloured man lay on the couch, a quizzical expression on his swarthy face as he toyed with a bullet Antonio had just dug out of his shoulder. He was from the Scrub Camp and had been shot in a feud. At times, hum pies were barricaded up there, and men were sniped at from behind trees.

Antonio's big son was one of the men from the Scrub Camp, he was quiet now but with the light of the devil in his eyes. Water-rights were mostly the bone of contention (sometimes native women were the trouble) in isolated mining-camps. This night the grave-faced men trusted me unquestioningly in their low-voiced discussion, my mateship with the Bairds being sufficient to ensure that no word of the affair would leak out to Cooktown.

I pushed out of the room right into the arms of Mee-lele. Her smile, her whispered "Jack-y" was sufficient; we were down the back steps and out into the cool of the banana groves. Mee-lele's eyes were wonderfully bright as she took the hibiscus from her hair and fastened it in my shirt.

"For memory!" she whispered, and kissed the flower.

Antonio's dance feast was gorgeous: roast sucking-pigs, ducks and fowls, fish. Granadillas, papaws soaked in wine creamed with sugar, sour-sops, mangoes, lichees, bananas, and custard-apples. Papaw, mango, and coconut wine.

At daylight, Antonio stood on the veranda and emptied his magazine rifle at the lightening sky. It was the signal. We left in merry boatloads.

12

THE CODE OF ASSAN RAH

WHEN eventually the trouble down south was settled, the weather took a hand; a sou'-easter developed into a raging blow outside. It might last a week, perhaps six. Against such a headwind the supply-lugger dare not leave Cooktown. So in resigned impatience we carried on with our food-hunting, and other little affairs.

Hearing that the alligators had made a raid on Mrs Ayres's goats, we borrowed horses from Arthur, swam them across the river and rode down towards the settlement, then turned up along the mailman's track that winds across Wyalla plain. Along this track the mailman jogged every fortnight, riding while he drove his packhorses ahead. It was a deeply trod track and so narrow and with grass so high that a man walking along it found the stalks rubbing his shoulders and the tops drooping over his head. Creeks coming from the mountains meandered across this plain and emptied into the river near the settlement. At high tide, a prowling alligator used now and then to swim up one or other of these creeks and scoff any unwary goat or dog. Tracks would occasionally show where at night one had crawled overland from creek to creek. A nasty thing to fall over in the dark is a twenty-foot alligator! That has happened too! Those were dangerous creeks at night, black shadowed by the tidal mangroves that lined them right out into the plain where they were overgrown with grasses and drooping forest trees .:

The waterholes were low and black, with, often, no sign of their presence until a man pushed through the grass almost into them.

We rode to the creek where the latest casualty had occurred and up along it until the grasses grew so dense that any beast would have heard the horses pushing through. Then Norman took the neddies away *out* on the flank while Charlie and I snaked our way through the grass, peering over at the pools, looking out for wallows, spying the little mud banks at the bends. Luck was with us, for we spotted an alligator lying on the mud with tree roots so thick around him that it was difficult to get a clear shot. The ugly brute lay like a Jog, his long jaws wide open and a little alligator bird busily picking between his beastly fangs.

We fired together and he rose against the roots, his forepaws outstretched as if to ward off a blow. Hard hit, he made a swaying rush down the bank but two more bullets stopped him just at the water's edge. He would eat no more goats nor be a menace to piccaninnies.

Quite pleased with ourselves we walked across to the horses, mounted and rode across the plain hoping to start a pig. The horses made heavy going of it through the tall grasses and shrubs, trying to keep their heads in the air and yet watch their knees against the hidden logs. A stream of travelling butterflies fluttered past like living flowers as they floated over two trees glorious under crowns of scarlet mistletoe. We started no pigs but heard the glossy starlings nearly two miles away. We rode across. Their home-tree was an unusual sight with its countless hanging nests; it reminded me of a trellised grape-vine overloaded with grapes. As we reined in, we could hardly hear ourselves speak. The big nests were neatly built of palm fibre, many so close together that the owners had hardly hopping room into their holes. It was the biggest, noisiest, cheeriest colony of starlings I had yet seen. Under the tree was a thick carpet of broken and blown down nests intermingled with a mass of partly eaten fruit.

"Don't go under the tree," warned Norman; "the old nests are alive with scrub itch."

That was sufficient. When a man gets scrub itch his fingers and toes become alive with microscopic red things that bore and burn him almost to madness. Kerosene and turps generally fixes them up – if the remedy is handy.

Several mornings later, the alligators nearly took a terrible revenge. We had taken the dinghy and with the early tide anchored downstream, fishing just past the little school. Hearing excited shouts we glanced upstream. The Olufsons' dinghy was coming, impelled by strokes that fairly lifted the bow out of the water, while the river echoed to that sharp ring of row locks straining against strength.

We leaped to the oars, for the oncoming dinghy had swerved in towards the bank, too hard pressed to reach the school landing. Youngsters came screaming down from the school attracted by the calls of the youngsters in the dinghy who sat perfectly still throughout so as not to upset the balance.

The old schoolmaster came running, calling wildly to some coloured men. As the flying dinghy crashed into the bank there rose up over its stern the long snout and huge forequarters of Big-nose. The youngsters leaped for the bank while the elder sister stood erect smashing an oar over that groping snout. He clawed in over the stern dragging it under as the sister leaped, almost too late for she nearly overbalanced as the dinghy's bows reared up. I t was a shivery escape. The Olufson youngsters walked the long scrub track back and forth to school after that.

Down at the settlement, things were quite lively. Several pearling luggers had run in for shelter from the blow. Low, rakish looking craft, the spray of the Coral Sea had lashed them from bow to stern. Half a dozen trochus cutters lay anchored there too, sails furled, a wisp of smoke coiling from the galley fire. Japs rolled cigarettes on the cabin roofs of the luggers while their dark-skinned crews cast longing eyes ashore. Saronged Malays paraded the cutters, and these went ashore just when they darned well liked, acting flash fellow with the dinghies, the Japs gazing on impassively. The settlement was animated with its visitors; some girls greeted lovers, others found new ones while the coloured youth of the settlement extended a guarded hospitality to the new-comers.

One afternoon I remember the girls were hilariously laughing because they had just thrown a big native seaman down the well. Some of those girls were as strong as young horses. A man was a fool who dared them to do anything. I never saw such a sheepish looking individual as that big sailor lad when his comrades hauled him up at the end of a rope. Though he smiled, his hot blood must have made him feel wretchedly small.

We lolled around Assan's house; some in hammocks on the veranda, others out in the gardens, the more privileged ones on the broad seats that encircled the trunks of the big, shady mango-trees. Cosy seats those were, sheltered even from the moonlight; what whispering intrigues have been hatched under those trees!

Assan sat, clad only in a pair of khaki shorts, carefully cleaning his rifle, his pig-dog resting at his feet. He was wearing the wizened little smile that seldom left him-in company anyway. He oiled his rifle lovingly and with painstaking efficiency.

Assan was a Moro man: he knew the Koran by heart. His father, whose honoured career as a pirate was history to all in the settlement, had taught him. He was a true son of Ishmael, a wanderer among strange lands and stranger people. He could tell entrancing, as well as terrible, stories of a life strangely foreign to our world.

Almost imperceptibly the people drifted away to gossip around the other seats, leaving me smoking beside Assan. He wrapped oiled calico carefully around his rifle-lock, laid the weapon aside, and reached under the seat. Then he sat back hunched up, his kris in his hand. The scabbard was of polished black ebony, glinting with pearl-shell disks; the massive hilt was inlaid with old silver; a shimmering baroque pearl adorned the butt. He drew the weapon and gazed dreamily at its bright wavy blade. The feel of the steel seemed to kindle a sympathetic throb in Assan's wrist. I stared apprehensively, for when a Malay runs amok he is a maniac.

"A serviceable weapon, Assan," I remarked.

"Yes, Jack. It has served my father, and his father before him." Assan sighed, his stubby brown thumb lingering along the blade. He stood up, stepped towards a banana-palm and with a light swinging blow sank the kris deep into the pulpy wood. He stood a few moments, then jerked it out and returned to the seat, staring at the blade.

"What for, Assan?"

"Look!" he held up the blade.

"I see banana-tree juice on it."

"Look closely!"

"I see nothing: unless it is that faint blue tinge like well-tempered steel."

"It is the poison in the juice," smiled Assan impressively. "It acts on steel. My people leave the blade in the tree all night. The juice soaks in."

"What for?"

"See, Jack," quite smilingly he laid the kris against my bare flesh. "This blade has been treated. If by accident I was just to touch the blade against your wrist-a scratch. Nothing! But--" and his hard eyes blazed-"in four months, in six, would come a sore, a running sore; sores would break out under your armpits, in your groin. There is no cure. You would rot away. In eighteen months you would be dead!" Assan sat back against the tree; the blaze left his eyes as he gazed down among the banana groves.

"Assan," I said daringly, "if you proved Mee-lele unfaithful to her father's bargain, what would you do?"

"I would cut her throat from ear to ear," he replied without the flicker of an eyelid. "I would carve her as I would a pig."

One afternoon I rowed upstream past Olufson's, intent on fishing at a favourite pool. I t was a place of bad repute; just where a narrow creek emptied into the river. Up that creek, where it narrowed between steep banks, a native spearman had been taken by an alligator. After such a happening that particular locality holds its reputation even though the incident happened long ago. The tribe had organized a moonlight wallaby batteau. The riverbank there is flat and grassy, with few trees except coconut-palms and mangrove. The natives started their beat from the foothills by moon and torchlight, a line of them shouting as they advanced down to··wards the river beating the grass and raising a hullabaloo. As they closed in, the two flanks hurried forward as horns which, when they touched the riverbank, enclosed all game within the semicircle. As the base pressed forward so the horns faced one another and advanced rapidly, closing a living pincers upon the wallabies which were now bounding in all directions as spears whizzed to an accompaniment of yells and waving of torches.

Growing excited at the rapidly approaching kill, one of the spearmen ran forward and attempted to leap the creek in front. He just missed the bank and crashed down in the darkness on top of an alligator. The beast grabbed him and the man snatched an overhanging limb screaming for help. In an instant the hunt was abandoned. The warriors rushed the place, but only dimly with the torches could they see the desperate struggle below. The limb broke away and they hopelessly slung their spears as the alligator rushed his victim down the creek and out into the river.

This afternoon while rowing towards the spot the sharp clout of stick upon stick suddenly sounded from the bank above. Investigation showed two naked lubras up on the grassy bank fighting with primitive fury, their mouths agape as they hit and parried while leaping aside to viciously strike again. Their weapons were fighting-sticks (long sticks of hardwood) and they used them with the agility of swordsmen, circling around one another and displaying consummate footwork while dealing lightning blows, each downward swing viciously aimed for the head. Eventually one received a glancing blow on the temple. She flopped to her knees as her antagonist leaped in and swung down a sickening blow. Her brains would have been dashed out but for that thick mop of never washed, clay daubed hair. It is this deadening pad which saves the lubras in their fights and when hubby chastises them with the wommera. In some tribes, when the lubras fight they stand up within the crowd and take blow for blow until one is knocked out. These two didn't, they sneaked away on their own and then flew at one another with no interfering rules.

This particular trouble was all over a certain young buck, a flash rider of Chulbil's, who strutted a big chest when told the lubras had fought over him. But I caught no fish, being softhearted enough to row the unconscious lubra back to camp.

At last the lugger was coming! Excitedly we listened at the Landing. From down-river sounded a confused bray of conches. Sharp eyes from a hilltop must have spied the *Pearl Queen·* away out at sea. She would anchor in the river-mouth at night and be towed upstream with the early morning tide.

Arthur sent his black stockmen cantering out to round up the horses. All was bustle, although pack-saddles were already sorted for the outward trip and the shed was piled with tons of tin, in little hundred-weight bags, ready for reloading the lugger. Norman, Charlie, and I were delighted, anxious to get back to our jungle camp, fired by the lure of gold. That evening we sprawled on the riverbank discussing things in general. Down at the native camp a blackboy blew monotonously on a yiki-yiki, a hollowed stick about seven feet long. Strong lungs are needed to blow it. Suddenly there came up-river a rumbling sound, like a distant bull lowing amongst timber. A native exclaimed "Big-nose!" We leapt to our feet, snatched rifles from the shed, and made off down the native pad along the riverbank. We emerged on a knoll overlooking the river that shone like dull silver in the moonlight.

Out in the river lay a long black log that as we looked rose and roared: it bellowed like a bull then partly submerged to spread up out on the surface again. Big-nose, thus almost fully exposed, appeared as sinister as his reputation. Charlie raised his rifle, but Norman said quietly:

"Wait a moment. Let Jack see how an alligator makes love."

The brute swung his head and tail clear of the water, his forelegs thrashing up and down as the powerful tail curled over his back to whip straight out and down. Again he did it, and the tail lashed up and over towards the snout-tip which was jerked high and back. He straightened violently to almost plunge clear of the water, falling back with a resounding splash. He whipped up his tail and smacked the river right and left. He rumbled in harsh coughing grunts as pivoting upon himself he tried to make a whirlpool. Then he lay perfectly still, his snout pointed upstream.

Norman grasped my arm and pointed. Ripples appeared, then the snout, the ridge over the eyes, the serrated tail, as the female swam out to join him. As she approached, Big-nose swung his tail to us and its lithe, twisting action headed him straight for the mangrove shadows on the opposite bank.

Charlie knelt down. He had a thrilling target, glorious moonlight, the whole bulk of the alligator though nearly submerged in line with us, the tip of his snout as a guiding line to the rifle-sights. Charlie aimed just back of the lumpy base of his head. The report cracked and cracked again up and down the river. The great tail of Big-nose swung straight up while his head rose to sink back. With a convulsive lash of the tail he plunged from view.

I was very glad, for Big-nose was due at any time to kill another human. It was his hard luck that he should be killed upon his wedding-night.

13

GOLD

IT always meant a lively two days after the *Pearl Queen* arrived: a stream of natives carrying the supplies from the lugger into the shed and reloading with bags of tin. Laughter and song, joke and hurry up and down the plank. A cloud of dust from the stockyard, clatter of slip rails, shouts of white men and black; big-eyed piccaninnies dodging the horses' hooves and the exasperated feet of the men; barking of dogs, hilarious laughter from the native girls as some luckless stockman was sent flying in the dust; prick-eared rogues awaiting their chance for a dash at the sliprails; dogs warily eyeing lively heels and prospective breakaways.

Just before we started out a coloured boy came up from the settlement, a knowing smile in his handsome brown eyes as he handed me a scented envelope. In it was a scarlet hibiscus. Mee-lele! How the little tease did love to bait the Killer of Pigs.

Norm and Charlie and I set out, yodelling farewell to friends and acquaintances, white and coloured. The tame cassowary, scenting movement in the wind, followed us for a while with stately tread, the wallaby hopping after, to sit back on his tail and prick his ears on finding we were taking the long track.

On the following stage from China Camp, we engaged natives to give us a hand up the mountains with our stores. It was a costly undertaking, for the good-humoured, chattering, surly, grim-faced beggars ate three times more than we. Luckily most of them would never camp more than a night or two with us in the jungle; it was *too* ghostly with "evil spirits."

We enjoyed a long spell on the highest forest peak, and sat gazing back towards China Camp. One felt the wonder of those mountains and valleys. There was Peter Botte with its tragic Two Sisters, and the massive bulk of black Alexander. The natives have a queer belief regarding that mountain. No native will venture within three miles of its base, believing that should he do so he will never return, for it is the home of the "Amazon Gins." They are a tribe of women of giant proportions and fearsome aspect who hate men and tear them to pieces when they catch them. These women can run twice as fast as a man, can jump twice as high, carry twice as heavy a spear and hurl it twice as far with unfailing accuracy. Should they chase a man he is liable to die of fright from their terrible yells alone.

However, even an Amazon cannot live forever, so to propagate their tribe they must, to their intense disgust, tolerate a few men. They have children, and watch carefully the growing boys. At a certain age the weaklings are seized and operated upon and are henceforth used as slaves. The operation is done with the phallic stone-knife. Only a selected few of the strongest lads are allowed to be men. These are trained as husbands, are fed and looked after with that express purpose in view, but otherwise remain in utter subjection.

There is much more but perhaps we'd better let it go with mention of a pastime of these women – the suckling of snakes. So attached do the reptiles become to their foster-mothers that when alarmed they crawl down their hostess's throat, to emerge again when she twitches her inside muscles.

The natives implicitly believe that the Amazons have inhabited the mountain from that far distant time when their own tribe took possession of the lowlands.

We plunged into the jungle, to find our track already overgrown with broad-leafed shoot and vine, creepers reaching arms across it, and tendrils curling down from branches above. Here and there a fallen tree had helped the job considerably. Charlie walked on ahead, slashing with the cane-knife. Cool and very silent was our jungle track.

Coorangy the cassowary gave me a fright and the natives a laugh on this particular morning. His curiosity must have been attracted by the sound of the knife. As he stepped out on to the track I bumped right into him. He shook his red wattles and bright blue neck and bounded straight into the jungle, leaping fallen logs like a racehorse.

Our camp looked very woebegone; plants were springing up in the clearing; the tent was black from mould and pitted with mildew holes. Night had nearly come so we put the billy on and set the natives scraping away the leaves that had rained on to the clearing, while Charlie temporarily rigged up the bunks. Some animal had amused itself by pulling them to pieces. Norman repaired the fallen galley and dispossessed a snake of the tucker-box. Next day the natives "borrowed" their final stick of tobacco, said a grave farewell, and trooped away *en route* to their beloved forest camp.

So we again sought gold, full of hope and the benefit of solid food. The occurrence of that gold was a fascinating study, in a meaning apart from our hopes and the intrinsic value of the metal when won. Learning from results gained after a number of trips to the jungle, it dawned on me that the gold was in tune with the pulsing life around. The more a man grows to know the jungle, the more the feeling possessed him that all life, everything, is one.

The jungle around just looked-jungle. But listen, seek, and you prove it a world of life. We never learned its secret. If a man lived a thousand years to learn it, he would still need a thousand more years. And the gold was part of its mystery; part of the earth; just as everything is. We found it first as wee pieces wedged tight in the fissures of the rock bars that jutted across the Big Creek. The upheavals of Nature, weatherings, gravitation, and finally rushing water had brought it there. From whence? How we tried to trace its source! How we surmised! How we tried to plan the mountains as they appeared millions of years ago, as a guide to where the gold was originally deposited. And how we worked! In between other trips throughout some years, we would return to seek again.

We found that elusive gold next in the terraces. Later still, I came with other mates. We traced it to a tiny creek running in from the mountain caps. After great labour we proved that that tiny creek had been a river in the ages before the mountain sides had tumbled down and squeezed it into the creek. Prehistoric creeks, of which all trace had long since been obliterated, had originally washed the gold into that one-time river. Like insects delving under the roots and trees and loam we carried on in almost despairing determination and eventually traced it to the mountain summits. There, right up on top of the world, we uncovered the remains of yet other ancient river-beds. But where had been the top of the world then?

Apart from attempting to solve the age-old secret of gold, or of where it was concentrated, and from whence it came, it was an extraordinarily difficult job prospecting that jungle. The labour and, above all, time spent in carrying our food there cut down our actual working-time considerably. Eventually we found a precipitous zigzag of ridges up which, in other trips not in this story, we each dragged a struggling, lightly loaded horse. Even so, when once at the jungle camp and unloaded, we had to rush the animals back to the outside forest, for there is no feed for horses in the scrubs. So much time occupied. Then the queries of the actual prospecting. Where to seek? Nothing but silence and gloom; the earth was covered with one vast network of roots; under that, two feet of decayed leaves; then feet of loam before even the real earth began. Where to look?

With the gold won, we would buy food for yet another search (two months passed as a rule before the food could arrive), or else we trekked away to the tin-fields for a change of life in the forest, to return with rejuvenated hope. The Queensland Mines Department generously helped us once; and in that trip we found our greatest river-bed only to find that portion of the age-old mountain itself had been washed away, or that some convulsion of Nature had pushed up another mountain in its stead and so displaced the bed. That particular trip aroused great anticipations and gave a few ounces of gold.

Those jungle ranges are a fascinating country.

They extend for a considerable distance along the northern Queensland coast; but the area which we regarded as our own started from Mount Fraser, near Mount Molloy, and ran straight north over the heads of the Daintree and Bloomfield rivers to Mount Windsor, where the scrub breaks into a sea of forest ranges, to re-form towards the coast in the Starcke scrubs. Tiny settlements are at the mouths of the Daintree and the Bloomfield. On the inland side of the mountains is forest country with cattle stations and mining-camps, made approachable by the wonderful climbing railway which, ascending the Barron Gorge, taps the rich Atherton Tableland. But our ranges stood in isolated grandeur. Approximately from twenty to thirty miles across, the only white man known to cross the jungle areas before this was Christy Palmerston, probably the most noted bushman northern Queensland has ever known.

By the fire at night, there on the Singing Creek, we often talked of the wealth that may be within the length of that magnificent barrier. In places, at least in the valleys and on the foothills and flats, the rich black soil would support future homes. There is timber too, awaiting the means of getting the big sticks out. But what intrigued us most was the strong possibility of mineral fields. The ranges are of granite, slate, quartz, and ironstone; geological conditions are perfect over a number of areas. Accessible mountains encircling the chain have long since been worked, Mount Molloy, Mount Lewis, Mount Spurgeon, Mount Carbine, Mount Windsor; the great chain of the Rossville tin-fields; the Normanby gold; the China and Scrub camps. And it is tipped by the Palmer, that Midas of gold-rivers. No wonder we used to think longingly of the heart of the jungle mountains. But to penetrate that heart-Ah!

Charlie had kept the camp in meat for awhile; now it was my turn to go ahunting. So come along with me. If you went with Charlie, you would meet with more success, but you might not learn quite so much, although Charlie is born with the eyes that see, the ears that hear, the instinct that knows. But he is a little impatient; often inclined to be silent; and perhaps would only smile when you questioned him.

When well away from the camp, I listened. Ears are assets when trained by the silence. No sound for a long time, then came little burring noises followed by the understandable deep bass call of a "Bolok-a-Blue!" pigeon. He would be hidden away in distant foliage, plump and fat and handsome, eating berries until he could gorge no more. The silence eases a little, insect voices break into it, faint little rustles, the tiniest of squeaks, hisses, and hums; each a distinct voice piping with the personality of its owner. A silken rustle on the bark of a tapering hickory betrays a long-billed bird encircling the tree in ascending hops. His hooked claws were designed to grip, his hooked beak to prise away the shreds of bark. His bright eyes now peering from cocked head are the very thing to spy insects hiding in crack and cranny. His coat too, of dark grey and yellow-green, renders him practically invisible against the bark. The jungle as a rule appears bare of birds. But it is surprising the numbers present in that roof of treetops where only the sun may see them; others in the lower foliage; different species again on the tree-trunks; other preferring the ground roots, the creeks, or the terrace labyrinths.

But this morning one heard no cluck of busy turkey, no rattle of stone or rooting grunt from hidden ravine to betray a fossicking pig, no rustle of bough to tell of a tree-climbing 'roo. Now and. again a soft "tap," that was the fall of a blue quandong, broke the silence. Presently I became aware of a long-drawn sighing that was not the wind through those massed tops above. I pushed forward to investigate, for the slope of the ground, the lighter built trees, told of the very lip of this mountain crown.

I shall never forget the sight. One step more and a man would have gone bounding and plunging amongst the treetops that spread from my very feet. I looked over valley after valley, peak after peak. Wind-blown mists were billowing above a sea of treetops. And there was a sound as if the world itself was deeply sighing. That was a vision splendid. It was with a strange subdued feeling that at last I turned back into our own small leaf of jungle.

When far enough in for the canopy overhead to dim that great sighing, I listened again. There came a harsh, throaty croaking, then the boom of Coorangy, my friend the cassowary. Again, he boomed, like a struck wooden drum. A tone in that boom told that he was not calling to his mate; neither was he moving over the country. Stealthily but quickly I moved in the direction of the sound, for cassowary steak is a dainty to hungry men.

14

COORANGY AND CHARAPENA

COORANGY the cassowary was having the fun of his life; exuberant joyfulness danced in his every antic. He perked and poked, toed and guggled, advanced in mincing gait to leap back in pretended alarm. He recovered to stretch his long neck to the ground, lay his head on a root, and stretch in a comical endeavour to peer underneath the queer fellow fastened there. He bristled his feathers, kicked out sideways while prancing in a circle, danced, ran, leaped as his merry throat croaked harsh remarks to something within that circle. He looked doubly handsome in his extreme good humour; mischievously bright were his bold, defiant eyes.

The horn helmet adorning his green-tinted head was a protective crown as his long bluish neck swayed in provoking taunt towards that curiosity curled on the ground. The glossy sheen of his blue-black plumage with its dense, hairlike feathers reminded me of Mee-lele's tresses. His throat and neck shone a cobalt blue touched with carmine; his eyes danced with fun as he waggled his head to sham a peck, only to leap aside in mock alarm. Coorangy was quite five feet high when he strutted out his chest and stood impressively erect, but now he could hardly stand still a moment.

The object exciting the cassowary's fun was a ball of formidable spikes, the yellowish, black-tipped quills of a porcupine. Fastening himself in between the roots, he thrust his queer pipe-like snout securely in under him, and protected it with ridiculously stumpy but powerful forelegs, bending them in under him to get a death's grip between the roots while with powerful shuffle and wriggle he jammed his ridiculous tail well in under behind. That quaint tail was the porcupine's tender and most vulnerable spot. Well he knew it. Thus he presented nothing but a bristling array of "touch-me-nots" to the mischievous cassowary. At every respite, when the big bird left him a moment, he got to work with his stubby strong legs, his toes armed with claws of steel and burrowed deeper into the earth with amazing rapidity, tearing roots, showering earth and leaves, actually sinking himself in as I watched.

The porcupine is an intensely interesting chappy, a ball of muscle who lives on ants mostly, licks 'em up with a tongue shooting out of his tube-like snout. He prowls about at night-time, and if you put your bare foot on him you'll wish you hadn't. When his wife presents him with a family she does it with an egg. And she hasn't a feather to fly with! Not unless her quills were feathers in the days when the world was young. She deposits the egg in her pouch, and baby is hatched right in the home with milk already laid on. But Pm not sure that he suckles; the natives have shown me how he bumps and paws at mum until the milk oozes through for him to lick. Baby thrives in his fruitful possy until his growing quills tickle mum uncomfortably. Then she tumbles him out and installs him in a warm burrow walled up and hidden from prying eyes.

Coorangy ceased his frolic. He advanced with solemn tread, his head bowing ridiculously to the uplift of his tail. He paused in contemplation; he stood over the porcupine; lowered his long neck and quizzed as a naturalist might study an insect. Tentatively he tapped a quill with his strong, dangerous beak; made an impossible attempt to peck the hidden tail.

Then he lifted one of those powerful legs of his and with the great claw arming his second toe, delicately scratched at the quills. They moved to the touch in a bristling mass. The cassowary leaped straight up in the air, coming down with a resounding thump to leap higher and leap again, twisting completely round in mid-air and kicking out with both feet at once. It was a striking display of lightning agility and bird humour. He scratched leaves in a shower over the porcupine and ran round and round it, his head low to the ground, chuckling hoarse, aggravating croakings.

A faint clattering of lawyer-canes instantly ended the display. The cassowary stood erect, listening. I listened. The porcupine had now almost completely buried himself and only the barked roots with a movement of damp earth and leaves showed where he was rapidly disappearing.

I smiled at Coorangy, genuinely glad of his reprieve, and quickly set off for that telltale clatter that told of a sow and her litter of rooting suckers.

That evening we lay in bunk, smoking the pipe of peace. Charlie lazily put his pipe aside and folded his brown arms behind his head.

"Who would live in the cities?" he murmured.

"You would," smiled Norman, "if you'd been born there."

"Pity we couldn't have two lives," I growled, "one for the city, one for the bush."

"Then you'd want others," replied Norman, "one for the sea, one for the sky, and one just to prowl around."

A fire-fly gleamed into the tent, and vanished.

"There are thousands of lives," declared Charlie.

"We might have lived all of them. That fire-fly lives in a different world to ours."

"I'm too comfortable to remember," laughed Norman. "My back just fits into this bunk so that I don't even want to think."

Our bunks were saplings, laid lengthwise, supported by cross-pieces on forked sticks. Thus we dodged the occasional snakes that crawled through the camp by accident or out of curiosity.

Sometimes, despite this precaution, a snake would crawl up the leg of a bunk and glide over someone's blanket. Then there was trouble, although the man who felt the snake waited, still as a mouse, until the wriggler crawled off him. Occasionally in the morning we would see a track that told of a snake crawling over a man's bunk and nobody waking up. However, snakes bothered us but seldom. And whether or no there are very few species that are dangerous. Bunks above ground were a safeguard against a far more dangerous menace – dampness ; and against a greater pest-stray leeches that came foraging across the bare clearing. Even so, a leech would occasionally pull itself up into a man's blankets, and from there work its way into his nostril, eye, or more tender spot still. They are dangerous then, especially the tiny, threadlike ones. They squirm their way down into the tiniest orifice and stay there, swelling up with the blood they suck. The best thing to do, if the least part of the leech is visible, is to heat a pin and apply the hot point to the pest. He backs out-lively. If you grip him he will cling to you with that suction mouth of his and you may tear some delicate membrane on which may form a sore perhaps hard to heal.

This was a happy evening. Charlie had got on to some promising gold in a new place farther up the creek and our hopes had risen like the sun. We had just enjoyed a gorgeous meal of fried sucking-pig and were healthily tired and happy. I had shot two suckers. One wore longitudinal stripes down his back, which Charlie assured me was because piggy's ancestors had slipped even farther back into the wild than his comrades.

A harsh, drumming boom echoed deep within the jungle. Norman laid his pipe yawningly aside.

"Coorangy must be 'tracking you to the camp, Jack," he murmured as he turned over.

The earth felt asleep, as if breathing deeply and gently, like Charlie. I was only hazily awake, not listening; dream murmurings of the jungle seemed drawing the I in me into the deep heart of things. Then came a deep sleep.

Utter confusion! Rip, tear, and bust! Clatter of pannikins, bumping of heads, crashing of bunks smacked by the billowing tent as all were dragged into a struggling heap.

What a frantic awakening as we pummelled each other and thumped against tent-poles and bunks! In suffocating alarm I burst up through the tent. Charlie was emerging swearing like a trooper-worse still, when he tripped over the tucker-box while hastening to the galley. Vigorously he blew the coals into flame.

Norman's dim outline was sitting up through the wrecked tent, a tucker-bag twisted around his neck. When he laughed I joined in wildly. Charlie swore with his mouth spluttering ashes. When the fire blazed up we searched for tracks. It seemed as if a thunderbolt had hit us; but we knew it must have really been the biggest old-man pig in all the mountains.

"Coorangy! " exclaimed Charlie pointing. "Blast him!"

It was the cassowary's tracks sure enough. He had crossed the creek, walked into the galley and pecked around a bit, then stepped into the tent. His imprints showed that he must have stood by Charlie's bunk quite a while peering down at us. Then he went right through the tent. I suppose he got frightened.

We put the billy on and yarned around the fire. We would have to build a new camp in the morning, a palm-branch gunyah. Anyway, the ruined tent was hopelessly rotted with mildew.

But we got even with Coorangy, just a week later. We followed his tracks from the soft mud of a creek into a dense patch of jungle, trailing a stub of mud here and there on the roots, just sufficient for Charlie's jungle-wise eyes. This jungle was oppressively damp, lichen clung like coloured skin to the tree-trunks. On a rotted log gleamed bunches of coral, pinks and whites in miniature branches, delicately beautiful. It was really a fungus beautifying Coorangy's garden home.

There was his nest, a few sticks and leaves scraped together at the butt of a magnificent Leichhardt tree. His wife had blessed it with three pale green eggs, larger even than an emu's egg. We ate them.

We put our hopes and energy into Charlie's new find. It was the lip of a tiny water-run coming into the creek some two miles up from the camp. Just a gutter, a convenient run-away for surface water during the "wet." But amongst its few stones was sand containing promising prospects of gold, each with a microscopic grain of quartz adhering. This meant a reef – somewhere! We were a bit excited, for each colour we got was more gold than stone.

But the lip only ran a few yards up the bank then tapered on up the hill, where it cut out. Try as we would we could get no further trace of gold here.

But it was there all the time; that is, traces of the great reef from which it came. After the war we returned to that spot, sank shafts down through the roots, ran deep cuttings through them and away, into the ridge sides below and found a great riverbed underneath with the same class of gold on its bottom.

But from what long vanished peak had this particular old bed washed its gold? If those trees could only have talked! That old river now lying deep under the roots of trees reminded us of buried cities we had seen unearthed in Palestine; cities the very names of which have been forgotten. Perhaps prehistoric men and women lived and loved upon its banks.

Coming quietly home one evening across a terrace flat we halted at a sound of energetic rooting.

"Charapena!" whispered Norman, as smilingly he craned his ear towards the sound. Stealthily we turned off from the path, Char lie edging in among the tangle, the born hunter showing in his lithe movements. Deep in among the lawyer-vines, Charapena was digging for yams. Usually he feasts on the treetops; but now with his hunched back towards us, he looked like a large fat monkey wearing a beautiful overcoat of yellow-brown. He was squatting on his tail; it was long and thick and black, and moved like a cat's when she scents a mouse. Charapena was evidently on a good wicket. As he rooted he grunted anticipatory grunts; he was getting near the yams as sure as Norman was getting near his tail. As Norman grabbed we threw ourselves right into the cyclone. A terrified squeal, rattling canes and laughter, then deep hissing grunts, a furry body heaving and wrestling with its eyes standing out of its head, striking with forepaws and legs armed with bear-like claws. The vines and Charapena's claws and teeth were too much for us. I grabbed a handful of pulsing body as he broke away to plunge like a terrified drunk through the canes and up a leaning tree in bark-shifting leaps.

He was a sluggard on the ground but an expert up a tree. He hooked himself out on to a limb and panting, glared down at us, his powerful forepaws crossed upon his paunch, his tail hanging down. A quaint picture of fright and outraged dignity, was Charapena the climbing kangaroo.

We laughed up at him and he spat towards us, hissing angrily, violently agitated, the fur on his nuggety little body standing on end. He had had a great fright, and made the funniest little go-away dabs at us with a muscular little forearm from which the tremendously developed claws stood out like curved hooks. Charlie heaved a stick up at him. He scolded back violently, his daintily pricked ears lending his pretty black head a comical expression of anger and dismay.

He gave us a fine Blondin exhibition along the limb then leaped agilely to the higher branches to peer again at us, voicing a hiss with a deprecatory wave of his forepaw. Hopping up so from branch to branch he was more agile than a climbing cat. It would be a long time before he came to the ground again.

We laughed our way back to camp, Charlie with a red face and a deep scratch where Charapena had boxed his ears.

15

THE HUNTERS

A WEEK of unceasing tropical rain came until everything looked so like rain that there seemed to be no air, just one soft hissing and the wet smell of vegetation and earth. The jungle was so misty that we could not see past the trees encircling the clearing. The swollen creek hurried past high over the moss of usually dry boulders, crashing over rocky bars to fall in a wind-blown boom into the gorge, thence over fall after fall on its way to the distant Daintree. The Singing Creek came tumbling down over rock and fern and palm-tree root, singing as ever though its lullaby was now an orchestra. Water was welling along every branch, pouring down every tree-trunk, dripping from every leaf; the lawyer-canes gleamed like the broad leaves of the water plants. The catbird was silent. The leaden light falling into the clearing was hours short in duration.

We lay in our cosy gunyah, telling yarns, yawning, making pick-handles, writing pars to the *Bulletin,* wishing the rain would cease. It was a beehive-shaped gunyah with one opening for door through which we crawled. Not a drop of rain came through the palm-thatched roof, for the Bairds could build a rain-proof gunyah as well as any native. We were not troubled for dry wood; we had the "kerosene" tree. This tree, though chopped down in rain, will burn almost as if it were soaked in kerosene. It is a surprising timber; perhaps the secret in its inflammable yellow heart may be of commercial or medicinal value. There are other varieties that burn easily when green, some as if sprayed with oil, but the kerosene-tree will blaze when a match is applied to a splinter.

When sunshine flickered through the mist we crawled thankfully from the gunyah and hastened to clean the clearing of its sodden leaves. Armies of leeches were now ranging the entire jungle, from baby ones like a thread of silk to gaunt whoppers three inches long. Bulging green and purple worms like slobbering snakes crawled up every ravine bank. Fungi in many colours, shapes, and beauty, shone and glowed on the rotted logs, and on live trees in the denser parts of the jungle. In our clearing, plants sprang up in the night, while the rich banks and islets of the Singing Creek reared countless seedlings in a fresh excess of riotous life. By night, the fire-flies were larger or their lights more brilliant as they skimmed into the blackness in pulsing whites and greens. The cat-bird called cheerily with the coming of the sun, imitating the scraping of our dishes, the knocking out of pipes; chuckling in cheeky self-regard as his perfect imitation attracted our attention and remarks.

The bush holds wonderful mimics in bird-life. Some feathered chaps can imitate numbers of things that walk, crawl, or fly. More than that, they can imitate inanimate things. I've heard a bird imitate a falling stone striking a rock, a tree-branch squeaking as the wind rubs it against another, the fall of a plum to the ground. A bower-bird near our camp used to imitate the knocking of a snail's shell against a rock. He had heard the chocolate heron doing that, when fishing along the creek. The heron would knock the snail against a rock to break the shell and get at the meal inside.

In a couple of days the creek had receded sufficiently for us to start gold-hunting again. We had been getting occasional 'weight up to five 'weight pieces in a ravine bed hidden under lawyer-vines. They were heavy little pieces of gold about the size of a large pea, highly payable if we could only have got enough of them. We tried hard to locate the lead from which they had come. We traced the yellow stuff half-way up the ravine; then it vanished as completely as if the yellow pellets had fallen from the sky. The place was hemmed in by gloomy ravine walls, matted with roots, and choked with an army of trees. To even guess the lay of the ground underfoot was impossible.

One evening when returning to camp we heard voices followed by a wild yell. When Charlie answered, tribal yells came ringing through the trees with dogs yapping a chorus. We emerged from the terrace pad to see a score of ochre-dabbed natives squatting in the clearing, carrying enough spears to start a small war.

They had come seeking Rungooma. They were boastful and excited about it; they knew the haunts he loved to root in after heavy rain; they were going to settle the man-killer this time. Their spear-points had been specially hardened, loose barbs removed and fresh ones bound on with wallaby sinew and grass-tree resin. They carried their heaviest hunting-spears and favourite wommera; they would camp with us so as to get a good start in the morning. That was their excuse anyway. The elders were dignified and quiet as befitted the wise ones of the tribe, but the younger men argued plan and counterplan. There would be something doing to-morrow! Norman put the billy on, chiacking the more boastful bucks as to how they would run should Rungooma be bailed up and charge. Charlie, too, poked good-natured fun at them as he washed the clay from his heavily muscled shoulders and jet-black beard. For we had grown beards on this trip. Mine was a curly brown. We looked wild and woolly, but we felt as strong as the big trees around us.

The tribesmen delighted in our ridicule. There was much poising of spears, much fitting of wommeras, laughter and grim jest. We knew perfectly well that this crowd had seized the opportunity of our presence to settle old scores with Rungooma. These were forest men. They were game enough in the forest, but would not have camped by night in the jungle had we not been there.

They "hummed" a bit. But then they turn up their noses when "white man's smell" is mentioned. They insist that we smell most disagreeably.

It was a big crowd that squatted round the galley fire that night, smoking our nigger-twist and lighting burnt-out pipes with glowing firesticks. All in great good humour. Hunting stories were eagerly listened to by the younger men, their eyes gleaming, spear-hands clenching at the inevitable "kills."

Night brought with it the jungle silence; a humming moth sped by followed by another swift and unseen; somewhere in the darkness a baby cassowary was crying piercingly. Charlie got more wood and fed the dying fire. All hands grouped closer round the blaze. Had the natives been alone, their fire would have been a mere smoulder. Now they squatted on their heels, hands loosely across their knees, staring at the fire, listening to the voices of the night.

After the hush, the elders spoke gravely, telling of the mystical things of the sky, the jungle, and the night. And all listened, staring at the fire with hardly a mumble in reply. Some of the things may not have been altogether mystical: the aboriginal is a fervent spiritualist.

In the dead of night I peeped from the gunyah. A score of black shadows lay coiled round the flickering coals, their spears beside them.

Morning dawned to great anticipations: it came within an ace of being the last dawn for me. We crawled out of the gunyah to the guttural news "Billy him boil!" and strolled over to the cheerful fire with the wide-awake warriors squatting around it.

We started off in single file. Three old warriors led, followed by Norman and Charlie, then a score of natives. I was in the rear, excited I'll admit at the possibility of witnessing a struggle at close quarters with the notorious boar. The natives were grimly in earnest; hunting is the breath of life to them and this promised to be a memorable hunt. Their naked bodies smelt of goanna fat; their shoulders were held slightly hunched as they dodged the vines, moving like black shadows amongst the gloomy trees. I was glad the ruthless beggars were on Rungooma's trail and not mine. The smears of pipeclay and ochre on their bodies merged them still more with the bark of the tree-trunks. I thought of those chaps a few years later, in the war years, when watching the camouflaged ships. Their long spears were carried effortlessly at the trail or half-slope as vine and timber required. The wommera only was in the right hand, a weapon and yet an aid as the warrior twisted amongst the undergrowth. I could see only the three men immediately ahead. The chap directly in front had enormous warrior weals standing out across his back;

his shoulder muscles were deeply scarred; feathers of the crane were in his arm-bands, a fillet of plaited hair bound back his shaggy hair decorated with tufts of cockatoo feathers. His buttocks twisted to the action of his panther-like tread and the muscles of his calves stood out like cricket-balls; occasionally I would glimpse the damp yellow-white of the soles of his feet as the leaves dropped off. Leeches clung among the hair of his legs.

During the noiseless halts, while the leaders were examining tracks or debating, those behind would scrape off the leeches with their wommera blade and methodically squash the crawlers against the nearest tree-trunk. Then on again.

The natives' dogs worked with an intense seriousness, noses to the earth, eyes gleaming, pressing silently on. Hideous mongrels they were, every knob in their skeletons protruded. Dogs that were fiends on the hunt, for they must starve or feast by the result.

After two hours stealthy travel we grouped up with the halted leaders on level ground, evidently the summit of a wide-spread, flat-topped mountain. Here; apparently, was a chain of mud lagoons, although thickly grouped trees made vision guesswork. The place was a spider-web of cable vines, some almost the thickness of a man's body looping from tree to tree like grey-green hawsers in the shadows.

All around us invisible springs were bubbling up from the very crown of the mountain. We stood on tufted mounds of reedy grass and even then sank slowly down. into loamy mud. Decomposed black logs lay everywhere, some partly visible under moss, others covered with creepers so that they looked like mounds of green stuff.

We stood listening, the dogs with heads outstretched, nostrils delicately inhaling, ears pricked and twitching to the air currents. Presently a soughing and a sighing told us we were on a mountain crown that dropped away into valleys.

We split up into two parties. Norman and Charlie's followed the swamp to where it would inevitably form the head of a creek tumbling down one side of the mountain. Half the natives and I followed the overflow in the opposite direction.

Pig-wallows and tracks were everywhere. Boars, sows, and countless suckers had rooted up patches like fresh ploughing in this rich bulb swamp. But no matter where they had rooted, the plants were growing again. Even where the rooting snouts had buried plants deep in mud, the leaves were pushing up again.

We kept a lookout for the larger wallows, for old boars usually wallow on their own, while the sows and suckers wallow in community bunches, sometimes even in little mobs.

We were climbing down over the lip of the mountain when we first saw signs of Rungooma – a huge wallow in blue mud as if a bullock had been lying there twisting himself round' and round, nosing and shouldering in slow, closed-eyed ecstasy.

Rungooma had only just enjoyed a luxurious bath of fine blue mud: he must be feeling all bucked up. His big tracks were fresh as paint where he had lumbered up on to solid ground.

In whispering eagerness the natives closed around those tracks pointing the" direction with their wommeras, their eyes already rolling at this tell-tale evidence of the quarry. The dogs nosed the tracks and trotted off in a business-like, silent mob. We followed after. It was a hurry-up scramble for me, sliding, slipping, falling, clutching at vine and root down that precipitous mountain side. A dog yapped excitedly away below, another gave tongue; then the mountain side rang with a fierce continuous yapping. Rungooma was bailed up!

They had cornered him on a level terrace close to a water-cascade. When pushing in through the tangles I noticed a snow-white wreath growing around the trunk of a tree: an occasional tree flowers like that. Cabbage-tree and fan-palms made the place look like an eastern thicket; rattans and canes looped the branches in coiling green ropes; a lone orchid dangled queer, snake-like blooms; and lawyer-canes in wire-like coils littered the root-covered, moss-hidden ground. The water from the cascade tinkled briskly; a fig smacked down as evidence of invisible pigeons in the foliage above.

It was a nervy place for an encounter with a wild boar, a gloomy, creepery, vine-entangled maze; no chance to run; no hope of leaping clear should he charge quickly. I noticed a moss-grown log bent up a little above the ground. Black men peered from behind tree-trunks, animal excitement in their eyes as they crouched forward, wommera fitted to spears that swayed as they poised seeking clear flight before the throw. The place was ringing with the vicious barking of the dogs.

16

THE BOAR'S LAST FIGHT

THE boar faced us with his rump and sides protected by the butt and wall-like flanges of a fig-tree. He was taking matters easy, grunting hoarsely at his tormentors. Snarling dogs barred his front, waiting for the spear-throwing ere they rushed in to the kill.

There was no handy tree slender enough for a man to climb if needs must, while there was so much vegetation in the way that it was impossible to make sure of a deadly shot. The natives were experiencing the same difficulty, as no matter how they poised their spears there was always leaf or shrub or cane in the line of flight. The quarry being at such close quarters meant too that they had only room for the short, jerking spear throw. What upset me most was the fear of hitting one of those snarling dogs. A man would have lost caste for all time had he killed a dog. A spear clicked with a sibilant hiss to be sharply deflected by a lawyer-cane to quiver in the tree. Instant yell of natives, furious barking of dogs as they rushed the flanges only to howl back from threatening tusks. Two spears hissed forward, one to thump swaying in a flange, the other to stick up they again leapt forward Rungooma shook them off with savage twists of his head sending one mongrel flying out among the palms. He grunted harshly to the yelping that rang among the trees. More spears flew, the natives stepped from cover, uncontrollably excited, fitting spear after spear to hissing grunts as they threw with the short arm jerk. They lost all caution, in the heat of the attack counting success assured by the whiteman's fire-arm. Then a spear struck Rungooma in the back and he hunched up to a surprised coughing grunt jerking up his snout and showing vicious eyes glittering from shock. He shook himself violently, while the bristles of his mane rose stiffly erect. The dogs leaped forward to the triumphant yell, snapping at his ears as in squealing rage he charged the scattering mongrels that leapt to get behind him, while others sought to grip an ear and, tugging behind his shoulders, safely hang on. j One mongrel's leg got twisted in the roots. His howl was awful, even before Rungooma was upon him ripping him from belly to throat, ramming him into the roots while the tribesmen raged. The boar thrashed around in slavering grunts as fangs nipped that tender spot below the tail. Shaking them like rats from his ears he wheeled back into the protecting flanges and faced around, grunting like a hoarse-throated bull, his jaws champing and slavering, his little eyes fairly dancing. A spear caught him in the neck and he shook himself, jerking his shoulders in fury as the barb held tight; another thumped into his flank and he came straight at us. I fired wildly among the scattering dogs and leapt aside to roll, heaven knows how, under that leaning log, hastened by Rungooma's snout and bestial breath. I pushed and punched at the slobbering thing as he rooted in and under trying to use his tusks. His snout thumped my ribs harder blows than a man's fist while what he was trying -to do nearly killed me with fright. He grunted gaspingly as two spears thudded into his side then twisted away in agonized squealing as fangs bit deep into that vulnerable spot behind. Dogs were all over him by then, spears jabbing down, thrashing of canes, and maniacal yells. But squeezed under that leaning log, scared stiff, I saw nothing of it.

My knees shivered as if fever-stricken when I crawled from under. Just as well a man soon regains his self-respect or he would never live to be a hero.

Back around the galley fire that night the tribesmen were in great glee, my party in noisy antic and pantomime going over the hunt again and again for the edification of their comrades. One good actor took my part, and brought down the jungle when he frenziedly rolled under an imaginary log. I had the doubtful compliment of knowing that for many moons to come mine would be the star part in the great native corroboree, "The Slaying of Rungooma."

A week later saw me away from the camp meat-hunting and full of pep again, but with ears keenly improved, at the least sound turning to listen apprehensively, well and truly "pig shy." Perhaps that was why I caught a muffled little tattoo, like a youngster's drum being sharply beaten far away. In the silence it recurred at intervals. It really was only three hundred yards away but the vegetation swallowed all but the tremulous hum.

When close, it sounded more a rapid whirring than a drumming, as if the drumsticks were tattooing feathers rather than a drum. Which was what the drummer was doing, his tautened wings stretched low to the ground vibrating rapidly as with cocked head and ruffled feathers he minced around in a circle. He was a spotted bower-bird, lost to the world in his job. He was not playing to an admiring lady either; or, if so, she was modestly invisible.

In a fairy clearing among the trees he had built himself quite a long tunnel of vines and twigs. Through this green archway he ran backwards and forwards, stretching out one leg then the other, his head cocked aside, his eyes quaintly serious as he rapidly clucked his piece. He hissed too and he put his soul into it. Both entrances to the bower were carpeted with fresh leaves, the light side uppermost, and spread amongst them were bright feathers, blue quandongs, snail-shells, and little specks of white quartz. I wondered if by any chance he might have specked a golden specimen. To the listening jungle he gave a ventriloquial display, mimicking quite a number of birds-among them our friend the catbird. I heard too the slow dreamy stirring of Norman's spoon in his pannikin – when we had any sugar. I even heard myself scratching a match on the galley hearthstone. I did not know that the bower-bird had spied on our camp. Perhaps he had borrowed the repertoire of that saucy rogue the cat-bird.

Time just dreamed on in the jungle camp, but not for the jungle. Time only held a meaning for Man. And man there was showing ominous signs. Soon our flour, tea, and tobacco would again be done; we had carried up the last of our stores from our depot in China Camp. Norman had sent away the little chamois bag of gold by the China Camp man-man to Cooktown, and soon we would welcome another trip to the Bloomfield to wait for the lugger. We were more than usually quiet in those long dreamy evenings. It was nice to sprawl smoking and watch the firelight playing on the nearest tree-trunks, to lose itself amongst the fantastic growths of the Singing Creek. But for that musical water, around us would be a heavy, brooding silence, as if all the trees were watching us. I have often felt that the jungle has a soul, a living soul too vast and terrifying to try and reason out. Norman's handsome face used to brood too. At times when his brown eyes became lost in the firelight I knew Melissa was smiling at him, laughter in her eyes, joy in her heart. But often Norman's thoughts were not of girls nor beings of the flesh. At such times in his intense brooding I could only imagine what he dreamed-perhaps of unseen things around, or of where the dead men go, or of why we could see on the Singing Creek the light that came from the stars.

Sometimes we awoke abruptly to a bloodthirsty, gurgling scream that rang out and choked, to scream again and wail among the trees. No matter how often we heard that "Death-bird" he always made our hair stand on end.

One evening, while hungrily devouring boiled pigeon and johnny-cakes with treacle, we glanced up at a noiseless visitor. He smiled down at us from a lean six feet of lithe manhood: a rifle in his hand, a belt of cartridges with sheath-knife around his waist, an oil-sheet with a very few things in it coiled bandolier fashion over his shoulder. His was a pleasing face, the restful expression emphasized by the quiet mouth and steady grey eyes.

We made him welcome; Norman insisted on giving up his seat (Norman's stump had a bag on it) but with a smiling nod the stranger squatted down on his heels and accepted the pannikin of tea. We knew instinctively that he was a jungle-man.

They are rarer than priceless orchids, but they exist, odd men who live on the bush. There is nothing "ratty" about them. The urge must be born in these men. Perhaps they are reincarnations of pre-historic ancestors. All of us, probably, have forest ancestors in the roots of our family-trees. The jungle may be more closely allied to man than we dream of.

I have met only three jungle-men. But there are some who roam the open forest (men who have gone right back to the wild), who really live on the bush. At times I have been forced to do that.

Various expeditions, when starting out, have said that they would live on the bush when provisions gave out. Only when the party consists of a group of men who have been in close contact with aboriginal life and know the more ordinary plant-foods and methods, often intricate, of preparing them is that possible. Even so, their time will be almost wholly occupied in finding food day by day. The bush is neither a larder nor a vegetable garden. What beats even experienced men who rely on the bush is the growing longing for flour and sweet things. The most sought after luxuries of the Australian aboriginal are the "sugar-bag" and honey ant.

Our visitor was a pure jungle-man – rarest of the rare. To camp one night alone in the jungle is a somewhat nervy experience. To live in it and make it keep you –!

I noticed a remarkable quality about our visitor's voice; he could make it distinctly heard quite a distance away without apparently raising it in the least. Sitting round the galley fire he was speaking softly and distinctly. I walked right across the clearing for some tobacco. At the tent I could detect his voice as a faint murmur; yet when I called to him his answer came with the same sort of distinctness as if I had been sitting with him at the galley fire. Another interesting thing was that when he answered me his voice sounded exactly the same to Norman and Charlie sitting beside him.

Among other things he told us that periodically he found the urge to return to civilization irresistible. That occurred once a year; for two months he would go down to Cairns. He enjoyed those two months as a schoolboy enjoys Christmas holidays. He found extreme pleasure in the simplest conversation; he was always ready to laugh; every phase of township life possessed an intense interest. In due course the jungle scrub called again and he returned quite alone. This man sought the "companionship" of the jungle; he delighted in exploring-in exploring the secrets of animal and bird and plant life. All those things "talk," he declared, if a man has the ears to hear, the eyes to see, the touch to feel, and can learn to respond to the "whispering voices." His own knowledge of these things was, apparently, inexhaustible. He roamed the jungle-land north and south, living on his rifle, trapping, fishing, and snaring. Strangely content.

In some distant range "towards the Carbine side" he had found "a gold creek" and he "had not been looking for it." He smiled at our expressive glances. He worked the hidden treasure only when he felt the "civilized" urge creeping on. He would never report his find; that would mean a rush, the cutting down of his beloved trees, the polluting of the creek, the slaying of birds and animals. While his find remained a secret between him and the jungle, he was the most independent man in the world.

"I may go mad," he murmured with that grave smile of his. "Perhaps I shall sluice out that creek then and go and live in the cities."

Apart from his periodical spells in Cairns the jungle-man had human company at intervals, for another jungle-man roamed the mountains a hundred miles south towards Cardwell. These two occasionally met and roamed together for a week or two. Their rendezvous was a valley where kauri-pine grew almost like a forest.

His nomad friend, too, was compelled periodically to return to civilization. At such times he would cut cane for several months during the sugar-season, down on the Mourilyan side. And he too enjoyed a wonderful two months with his fellow men until the jungle called again, when he would disappear in the night. This man complained of the money he had made. He did not know what to do with it!

Our visitor stayed with us some time. From him I learned jungle lore that I had never dreamed of. "Books in the running brooks," indeed!

17

THE FILIPINO

RETURNING to the Bloomfield we found everyone happy, as usual. There had been one or two new babies amongst the coloured people, so Chulbil assured us, but "nothing to talk about." A carpet-snake had scoffed five fowls from a hen-roost; the new alligator had mauled the mailman's saddle-horse; two niggers had been speared; "The Coon" had stopped a bullet up at the Scrub Camp; otherwise there had been nothing much doing. So we borrowed two bags of flour and sat down to wait for the lugger. It proved another long wait. Meanwhile the river people lived on beef, sweet-buks, and bananas.

A picturesque crowd of sea-rovers were "spelling" at the settlement-the Pitt families-their vessels anchored out in the stream. The Pitts were tremendous men, huge brown fellows, following the sea as pearlers, trochus shellers, and *bêche-de-mer* men. A few years later the families made Cairns their headquarters, from whence their fame spread over all the North as probably the greatest swimmers Queensland has known. Few coastal Queenslanders at least, do not know the stories of their wonderful swims; sometimes in cyclones, for several days and nights in a raging sea, the different brothers and their womenfolk swimming twenty miles and more while keeping afloat coloured people or white; and other feats-epics in the human history of the North. The Cairns people talked of sending the Pitts overseas to swim the Channel but the project never got beyond that stage.

However, the Pitts were unsettled rovers at this time when they anchored in the Bloomfield. I was glad of their presence, for in the communistic mix up in the settlement the presence of so many somewhat arrogant strangers diverted attention from Mee-lele and me.

I do not mean that the coloured people were typical communists. On the contrary, except that they lived in what we loosely call a community system, there was no communistic business amongst them. They believed most definitely in individual ownership, in caste, and in religion. For the rest, they were an excitable, fightable, intrigue-loving crowd. Hospitable to a degree, always ready with the helping hand, yet their lives held numerous bitter rivalries and jealousies. Not only over women. Centuries-old feuds from overseas continued here. And money matters and sea rivalries provided apples of discord.

Mee-lele let me know the real men and women that lay behind the smiling faces, or grim, of every man and woman in the settlement. She loved to gossip.

Poor little beggar, Life had been cruel in making her a coloured girl, crueller still in educating her and then thrusting her back under the iron rule of her people.

"But I'm not married yet," she would laugh.

"Why don't you run away with me, Jacky?"

"Assan and his dog would track us as they would a pig, Mee-lele."

She whispered, "I know you can't, Jacky. You are a white man and I am a coloured girl. We are only playing, you and I."

Mee-lele's home and her childhood friends were at Thursday Island, four hundred miles farther north. She had been brought here (for surety I could guess) to await the marriage, guarded by her brothers. She could hardly have been more isolated, more at the mercy of her people and their customs, had she been on an islet in the Coral Sea. She had tried, so Chulbil told me, to coax a Jap pearler to give her a runaway trip to Thursday Island. But the Jap, though he will risk his own skin in an amorous adventure, will never do so should there be chance of trouble with the authorities later. With the Jap's wonderful patriotism, when in a foreign country he will do anything rather than bring the least slur upon his country's name. Rather than that, he would commit suicide.

I gradually developed a conviction that Mee-lele was working towards some desperate plan, a last-minute plan, and intuition told that the Filipino was in it. I had never seen this mysterious sea-rover, for the simple reason that he dare not show himself within the river. Arthur told me he was a *bêche-de-mer* fisher, a black-moustached, savage-looking chap, a seeker of the sea-slugs that make the soup for the Chinese mandarin's table. A shadowy sort of customer, his name was *tabu* apparently to all the coloured folk in the settlement. They would laugh his name away if inadvertently mentioned. But this hardy sea-rover could not have been altogether a joke, for he had defied the whole crowd of them and came within an ace of getting away with it. In his little five-ton cutter with a crew of four he roamed the Coral Sea from the Barrier to the Gulf of Papua, and round Dutch New Guinea to the Aru Islands. He could handle a cutter night or day through uncharted waters and knew all about looking after himself. He had tried to run away with Mee-lele at Thursday Island, only her own dilly-dallying had messed up the elopement. Her dusky Lochinvar had his cheek slit open by a knife, thrown by one of her brothers, as a memento.

Mee-lele flared up, then burst into passionate tears when I asked her about the Filipino. For some reason I was the last person in the world she wanted to know of the man. Privately, I began to wonder whether she was in communication with him. That was quite possible for the native seamen who occasionally visit the river all love an intrigue, and during their cruises out to the Great Barrier Reef they would be sure to sight the Filipino's cutter hovering about – if he wanted them to sight him.

Again our stay on the Bloomfield developed into months; the supply-lugger, due day after day, failed us week after week. We spent the time happily as usual; gave the Pierces a hand occasionally with their cattle in the back country, or fished, hunted, or loafed.

Though initiated on an earlier trip to the Bloomfield, I sometimes mused on the unspoken code rigidly adhered to in our separate little feminine friendships-quite innocent though they might be. We strictly minded our own business. We were great mates, all of us at the Landing, a happy crowd, but we must never interfere in one another's flirtations. We each knew in a roundabout way what the others were doing; only the individual himself knew the particulars. We might indulge in light personal banter occasionally, but must never question or pry even in a friendly way. Any stranger to that little community, even though he might live there awhile, would pass on, quite unaware of the social undercurrent that flowed beneath several phases of the life there.

Arthur, apart from an odd joke, always kept strictly aloof. He was deeply in love with a white girl. I don't remember more than half a dozen white girls of interesting age on the river; but they were a splendid type of young womanhood. Like Arthur, they generally kept aloof from the coloured people, in a nice quiet home-life. It was to the more accessible, and I suppose "livelier," people that we other four used to pay our attention.

Quite apart from the age-old lure these latter were very interesting. I loved to listen to the grave-faced elders telling true stories of adventure by land and sea; of savage people practising fearsome rites on coconut-strewn isles; of still more fascinating under-water stories of "dead" ships and the weird life deep down amongst the coral gardens. Stories, too, of the teeming life of the Malay Archipelago, of the South Seas, of pirate proas and villages; of long drawn out fights against the Dutch; of native princes and Court intrigues; of desperate but courageous white castaways who had held to life against dreadful odds and carved out a name and a memory there; and other stories.

The Malay element, particularly, believed in the weirdest of weird superstitions. On the verandas during the quieter evenings those grave old sinners would tell stories and beliefs that made my hair stand on end. Not only did they believe in conversation with and bargains with the spirits of dead people, they believed implicitly in animal ghosts, things half animal, half bird, that had lived when the earth was young, and later things half human, half animal, that must have given contemporaries the nightmare. The realistic details left little to the imagination. But these things could be seen only by certain men and women who possessed what we call second sight.

Specially gifted and trained men among them, I was assured, can under certain conditions and at certain times, influence both human and animal spirits to do their bidding.

Not the least surprising thing about all these beliefs was that there was not an unbeliever in the settlement.

Alligator teeth, eggs and nest.

18

THE SKELETON

OCCASIONALLY we listened to the stories of the local native romancers. These serious-minded folk are keen on story-telling and play-making: they think out a picturesque plot, too, occasionally, as befits born actors and mimics. They have wonderful memories and an eye for natural, comic, or dramatic detail. Some of these fellows build up inter-tribal reputations. And their stuff, if presented as authentic, *has* to be authentic for the author is surrounded by critics who know. More than once we have heard a story-teller sharply contradicted when he strayed from the strict truth, or misnamed a weapon or locality, a bird, beast, tree or fish, or a man. Occasionally a debated incident would develop into a furious argument which, when the narrator was called a liar, would end the story in a wrestling match, with skin and hair flying if Arthur were not about. The natives think highly of their "authors," which is decidedly in their favour from my point of view.

A native story-teller who can think out a good "play" for the seasonal ceremonies, and get it acted, has not to go and dig his own yams. His royalties come to him, so to speak. In addition to their immemorial ceremonial and seasonal dances, initiation rites, totem and story dance and song in connection with tribal customs, they weave stories of love, fighting, adventure, humour, and tragedy. But they are especially keen on nature and "spirit" stories. I am not alluding to the absurdly childish stories they generally retail to white men.

It was on a story-telling night such as this that I first heard of "the silver show." In the middle of the particulars a piercing scream rang out from the native camp followed by the barking of dogs and furious voices.

"Someone's getting his head broke," laughed Chulbil. "I'll bet a pound of Capstan to a firestick there's no corpse."

There wasn't. Only a buck with a spear through his ribs, thrashing among the bushes like a transfixed wallaby. He had been courting another buck's girl.

To break the monotony of life, the three of us decided on a fortnight's "walk-about." We would go and investigate the silver show. This show is a campfire story on the Bloomfield, of a silver lode located some years ago. The blacks were then "bad;" transportation in bulk impossible; prospectors were looking for gold, not silver. They found the show only to abandon it.

Returning to Cooktown they had sent away a few specimens which returned a rich assay in silver.

I cannot say if the lode actually was found. Anyway, there was an old nigger on the Bloomfield who had been one of a party who attempted to spear the prospectors when they were working "out there." So with him and his mate as guide, Norman, Charlie, and I set out, walking and carrying one blanket, rifle, a bit of flour, tea, and sugar. For the rest, we could easily enough live on the bush.

It was an interesting walk-about to the north of west, amongst a sea of tangled hills, grass covered and rocky. At sundown we camped just where we were, generally choosing a scrubby creek having a sand-ringed pool in among its trees. It is always easy and comfortable to sleep on sand, no sticks or stones or stubby grass-tufts to get into one's ribs. And if it is cold, one can always scoop out a shallow trench, line it with sweet warm grass, and sleep comfortably, protected from the wind. Bush rats and quite a number of other things line their burrows that way. You have no idea how comfy it is. Besides, on sand, there is little chance of spreading your blanket over a snake hole, as Norman did one nigh t. There was an unpleasant brown snake in it too, that evidently had business abroad, for it managed to wriggle out of the hole. Just at the critical moment Norman rolled over and enlivened the reptile so much that Norman awoke and nearly landed in the fire.

Occasionally, we found a quiet creek pool swarming with fish. They were not large, but they bit like young sharks. We would pull the beggars out right and left while the niggers bit off their heads and threw them on the coals.

Nights were quietly pleasant: it is nice to be happy. The firelight playing on the water-pool; the wood bursting into a warm little crackling; a cricket chirruping; the open forest around and the stars above made us contented with the world. Healthily tired after a hard day's work we would lie there and smoke, listening to the wrinkled-faced bucks telling tales of the days of old. Their low, murmuring voices would gradually rise, their watery eyes light up, their grey-haired chests breathe deeply, their spear-hands tremble as they lived again the days when they could spear a man and eat his kidneys. One night in the heat of an absorbingly bloodthirsty story a piercing scream electrified us, followed by swishing wings that suggested the Angel of Death himself. A plunging instantly followed by a pitiful screech made our blood run cold as we stared into eyes of molten gold. Upon the sand by the firelight edge the winged hunter of the night had him down, curved talons deep in his flesh.

Over his victim the Powerful Owl glared at us. He was terrifying but superb in his bloodthirsty strength; he looked three feet high in his bristling feathers. The deep yellow talons of his short powerful legs mercilessly gripped a baby wallaby. His great hooked beak partly opened as with raucous screaming he brought his heavy-shouldered wings down on his prey and buffeted it flat on the ground.

Then with a shrug and whouff! whouff! whouff! of great wings he bounded up and was gone.

Our following day's walk was a stiff climbing up and over ironstone ridges heavily timbered with ironwoods. Deep down in one of the innumerable dry creeks a slender branched acacia-tree appeared loaded with birds' nests-really the nests of green ants. Our natives made down the ridge towards this tree, evidently feeling the need of a little ant juice.

Those green ants are so lively they fall over themselves trying to bite anything that trespasses near the tree. Walk under it, and they fall on top of you, sink their nippers in, double up their backs for a grip, and cling. Branches, leaves, and twigs swarm with the aggressive green terrors. They are efficiently organized fighters and builders, putting science, brains, and brawn into all they do. Wonderful team workers, not a loafer in the crowd. They pull a bunch of leaves together, cement them, then hurry on with the domestic business inside. On every branch crowds of them are busy making nests. This is how it is done.

A big gang will select a branch on which the twigs are fairly close together. Then the "heave-ho!" gang swarm out on the twigs and man the closest grouped leaves like old-time sailors swarming the yard-arm. Shoulder to shoulder and back to back they grip the edges of the selected leaves and tug and jerk, pull and scratch for a foothold like sailors tugging at the sails in a storm. Next, out run the chain-gangs, adding their scientific weight to the pull until the leaves are drawn close together. All hands now hang on desperately until the leaf-edges are sewn and cemented fast. The nest is gradually formed in football shape with the foundation leaves. These laid, or rather glued, the big mob don't take a breather; they merely gaze panting at how far away the next leaves are. Then they rush on with the job. They swarm out to a distant leaf; a stout fellow gets a grip on its edge and hangs, his hind-legs wobbling desperately in space. A mate climbs down his body hand over hand, slews around and gets a grip on his waist at the same time that another worker is swarming down over both of them to get a grip on number two's waist. So they form a living chain from this leaf right down to the nest. During building, these chains, sometimes, look like wriggling bits of greenish-brown string. It is comical to see the builders down at the nest reaching out to grab the last man on the chain. Sometimes a light breeze sets the chain swinging in mid-air. Then there is hell to pay until the bottom chap's rump bumps some twig or other, or is caught by an agile toiler reaching from below. Immediately the chain is grabbed, up along it swarm other ants to form 'another chain and add their weight to the pull. Often, there will be a number of these chain-gangs battling to bring the outside leaves down to the nest. Once the first chain is anchored all hands seize it and haul desperately. There is a devil of a pull to get the twig to bend sufficiently before the leaf is in place, and when the leaf is finally hauled down to the nest, they must hold on like grim death until the leaf is fastened. They manufacture their own thread and cement, or rather they breed it in their larvae. While the mob are still straining and tugging with the leaf-edge in position, trained workers come along carefully carrying the little white grubs and take their positions in among the chaps holding to the leaf. The grub is shoved against the leaf-edge and coaxed or forced to sew the leaf-edges together with a cobweb-like, sticky thread he unrolls from his mouth. The threads from these grubs are formed into a "spider-web" which not only fastens the leaves but in some cases covers the big completed nest like a filmy silk veil finer far than human craft' can make. On dewy mornings these veiled nests sparkle with a million diamond points.

Our natives weren't interested in nature study, however; theirs was the universal urge; they merely wanted to "eat up." In a lively, skipping hurry they broke down half a dozen of the lower nests, flung them well away and ran, brushing a horde of ants from their heads and bodies. Finding a tiny rock hole they cleaned the sand out, filled it with water, threw a nest in and squashed it down with sticks until the mass was broken up. Then, throwing out the numerous leaves they treated the other nests similarly, I was graciously invited to take the first drink of squashed ants, pupae, shreds of leaves, cobweb, bits of stick and grass. The drink, when properly mixed in a clean kerosene-tin, has a nutty, acid taste. It is not bad, but I'd prefer a pot of beer any day.

As we drew near the mountains the going became much rougher, the hills rugged and abrupt, trees growing out from among the rocks, clinging even to the ledges. Brown hawks appeared miraculously from out the sky, making for the rising smoke where we had set a hillside on fire. The hawks dived into the smoke after dazed things that sought escape, just as the smoke-blinded wallabies sought escape from our natives.

Our intention was to skirt the edge of the mountain range only, but a valley leading into the range was tempting to explore. A stream, more boulders than water, trickled through it. Some lovely trees in heavily foliaged groups from which flocks of parrots noisily inquired our business, grew along the valley. But what interested us was the "timber," beautiful sticks of cedar, hickory, and pine. I don't know whether there was much of it, for we didn't go far beyond the mouth of the valley. Our boys were unwilling. According to them, an old man devil dwelt there and had cast a hoodoo over the place long ago.

Our guides eventually led us up a granite hill.

"It's like climbing the walls of a broken down castle," said Norman.

It certainly looked so, gazing up from a mass of tumbled boulders. We got our breath and climbed on. A breath-taking view of rugged grandeur rewarded us from the top. Hills all around that only a mountain goat would enjoy climbing. On one side a mountain loomed right over us. These were forest mountains covered with sheer grass slopes and forest trees.

The natives pointed out a mass of black rock as the "silver." It was a lode right enough, ironstone, but we could find no silver in it – not rich anyway. As we gazed over the country we longed for a pack-horse team loaded with tucker. Those untrod hills of granite and slate, ironstone and quartz, seemed to be calling for the prospector.

We lazed along on the return walk to the Bloomfield, "knapping" any likely looking reef we saw, and hunting for food. Almost every scrub creek homed its turkey or two; some creeks had fish-pools; edible bird-life, pigeons, cockatoos, and parrots abounded. And carpet-snakes, wallabies, and kangaroo rats and witchetty grubs provided plenty of food for the two old abos. And yams were there for all.

This country was richly historical for the Bloomfield natives. Our bucks knew literally every yard of it; it had been their tribal grounds from time immemorial. Charlie pointed out one rugged little landmark, a mass of grotesquely shaped rocks like a knob broken in fragments from the side of a spur, with a clump of small but heavily foliaged trees clinging to it. Among those rocks lubras would sit for hours, waiting for a "spirit" baby. Any woman who wanted a child, waited there. The tribal ancestors of semi-god, semi-human relationship of long ago had left on that spot the spirits of countless children for the future of the tribe. Consequently, if a woman wanted a child she went there and the child-spirit entered into her. Naturally enough, numbers of lubras avoided the spot like the plague.

Sometimes when a creek was running our way half the party would walk one bank, half the other so as to see game if it emerged on either bank. Game feeding or hiding in the creek itself would thus probably run or fly into view of one party or the other. As one of the natives and I were dawdling along in this way, he told me of the innumerable whatnots that make their home in ant-beds. Some of these beds house a remarkable alien life inside their sunbaked walls. Lesser things of the wild that are bitter enemies outside camp side by side with only a shell of dug-out galleries separating them.

A big ant-bed, fully twelve feet high, heavily buttressed like a medieval castle, stood out fairly crying for the test. There were some parrot holes in it, and the burrows of other creatures. Very unwillingly my companion handed over the light prospecting pick. As I dug it into the nest he tried to draw me away with the solemn warning that the others would be far down the creek and we would be lost. This provoked me to dig much farther into that big clay heap, and the farther the pick dug the more uneasy he became. In among those countless galleries there certainly were other living things besides the confused ants. A stroke of the pick wrench away the toe-bones of a dead thing just as I was about to desist.

Careful picking revealed the skeleton of a man sitting there with his knees under his chin; the ants had long since built their galleries through his ribs and in his skull. It would have been a long job to have dug him out; he was walled in and through and through with clay. The pick had snapped an arm-bone and several ribs as it was. The snapped bones showed quite white but minutely honeycombed; otherwise the bones so far as could be seen were a deep yellow-brown.

I understood the reason for my companion's reluctance.

Natives had partly dug out the nest and propped the corpse in long ago. The ants of course would immediately set to work to re-close their nest and they work with phenomenal rapidity, especially after a shower of rain.

In later trips farther north, I found similar and even queerer resting-places of the dead.

I wanted to know why he had been planted there; whether he had been a corpse, or eaten first, or even been alive when they fastened him up in there. But the old native shook his head, denying all knowledge of the deceased.

Perhaps they killed him because he knew too much. He may even have been a white man!

19

THE JUNGLE WINS

WHEN at last the *Pearl Queen* arrived, she had "short orders" aboard for all hands. The Cooktown storekeepers had themselves received short supplies, hence had rationed outside orders. This meant a serious difference to us three gold-hunters. After repaying the stores borrowed we had only sufficient left for a short stay at our prospecting.

Mee-lele said a tearful farewell, not crocodile ones either. I had grown jolly fond of the girl and felt a bit afraid of the ultimate result. Mee-lele was a lovely girl, yet she was so very human, and had been awfully nice to me.

I'm in Sydney now, and occasionally think of Mee-lele when watching a screen beauty "do her piece" in some wild and woolly eastern picture. Occasionally the actress does look something like the part. But Mee-lele was the girl in the warm, living flesh, a living picture of the moonlit girl in the palm-tree setting.

I promised Mee-lele that I would return for her wedding, some months hence. She made me swear so by the white man's most sacred oath. Then the ever-near smile shone from her tear-dimmed eyes, the devil's mischief from the little face.

"You will come, Jacky; you love excitement. Assan will never forget his wedding-night-neither will you!"

On the long trail up to the jungle camp I pondered Mee-lele's last words. The more I thought of them, the stronger grew the feeling that Assan was due for a shock.

We set to work in a hurry to locate enough gold to buy a further six months' provisions. We had little time to do it in. To eke out our flour we had brought along three bags of sweet-buks. They are a change and a splendid substitute when fried for either meat or bread. Men who dine on fried sweet potatoes alone, can for a time at least be satisfied without either meat or bread. To make our salted, and small stock of tinned, meats last out, one of us was continually raiding the jungle for pig or turkey, pigeon or climbing 'roo or crayfish. The slaughtering of those poor old crays was amusing.

Little colonies of them lived in the crystal-clear pools under the rocks in the big creek. They would come out and scout around on the sand and pebbles of the pool, looking quite lively, wide-awake creatures; ready to back under a rock at the threat of overwhelming odds. We caught them with the leaf of the lawyer-vine. Its rib is armed with a formidable array of needle-pointed hooks set one after the other, worse than the barbs of a fish-hook. The point of the tough rib is as sharp as a needle. We would cut a leaf, strip the long barbed rib and lower it into a pool, waving the point gently to and fro just under the lip of a ledge of rock. Now, the cunning green crayfish imagines he is perfectly safe under water. So he would be, if he were not so curious. He pokes out his head to inspect the stick, and gazes up at us. We move the stick gently, tantalizingly, withdrawing it from the rock as the crayfish stretches out his nippers. He comes out from under the rock; we offer him the point of the stick; tentatively he reaches for it first with one claw, then the other. Very gently we move it. I suppose the crayfish imagines it is alive, something to eat. Anyway he obligingly carries that needle-point straight for his mouth. When we see his "whiskers" moving we know he is "set" and thrust sharply but not too hard. The poor old thing has swallowed the point and first barb. He kicks frantically, but is hauled out and dropped into our billycan to compare notes with numerous disillusioned mates.

It was while cray-fishing that a rifle-bird gave us a beautiful exhibition from the terrace bank opposite. His wild, excited cry drew our attention as well as the attention of his devoted mate. She watched him adoringly as he showed off his paces, dancing, bowing, and turning his head to every point of the compass. His velvety plumage was like a polished black glass reflecting the colours of the rainbow; faint blue, rich purple, vivid green, polished steel, and a flash of chocolate greeted the eye as he danced and bowed. Probably he can only produce that gorgeous colouring under his ecstasy of love-making. His mate's soul seemed to be in her eyes as she adored him.

"Come and have a look at the nest," said Norman. "It is almost as striking as the bird itself."

It was, for hanging from it were the cast-off skins of snakes, barbaric tassels to the home of a beautiful bird. The rifle-birds generally adorn their cleverly hidden nests with these skins; they regard them as ribbons perhaps, for quite a number of birds have an eye for ornament. More likely, they realize that those skins will scare birds of prey from their nestlings.

The big fruit-eating pigeons always helped us out. They were always so plump; a single bird, at times, would make a meal for one man. There are a number of varieties, and the plumage of some rivals Joseph's coat for colour. Our hunter had to locate the bird first; listen for the deep bass call; then find the tree; a puzzle indeed in that sea of timber. Guided by our ears and using our eyes, we looked for the ring of berries or fruits at its base.

A 22 rifle is the most efficient for pigeons; a '32 Winchester for pigs.

Finding the tell-tale ring only half finished the job. One then walked slowly round and round the tree, his head well back between his shoulders, staring and peering, back-stepping and side-stepping, ears as wide awake as his eyes, trying to glimpse a purple breast amongst the dark green leaves. At intervals, the bird above would call in hoarse-voiced complacency. Now and again a fig came dropping to the ground. A flapping rustle up there made the hunter's heart beat, for that meant a number of pigeons. Lazily they would flap from branch to branch among the leaves. Sometimes, worse luck, with their crops bulging like balloons they would squat there comatose for hours. Often they would not fly at the report of the rifle, which meant that a deadly shot might get a meal for three men from the one tree. But there have been times when I have stared my eyes out and then had to return to a hungry camp empty handed. And probably all the time a fat pigeon had been sitting up there not knowing or caring about the danger lurking down below.

We never went short of pigeons in the jungle during the nutmeg season. Then the Torres Strait pigeons would come in clouds from the islands to feed on scrub and jungle fruit. They would settle in flocks on practically every nutmeg and scrub fruit tree. Beautiful cream-coloured birds, with tips and tail black, they were a little larger than our domesticated pigeon. In the evening, again in clouds, they would fly back to the coastal islands where they breed.

But the jungle beat us. By the time our flour, tea, and tobacco was exhausted we had won a few ounces of gold, but not sufficient. So Charlie sprang us a surprise. He suggested we go down to the Mossman. The cane season had started. There would be plenty of work in the cane-gangs. We could knock up a big cheque quickly; see new country and people; enjoy a change of life and civilized food; then take the steamer back to Cooktown and – he added while staring at the fire, "be back on the Bloomfield in time for Mee-lele's wedding."

What had been brooding in Charlie's mind I don't know. He was inclined that way; he would think his thoughts and only tell them if he wanted to.

As a rule we went "tin scratching" as a means of replenishing the commissariat. We never liked wages work. Since we had been mates we had never tackled it; we were always our own master. But Charlie's scheme was new and attractive. Above all it was a change! – a change from the gloom and quietness of the jungle to far-away civilized life with its company, its talk, its meals, its noise – its everything!

We decided immediately. We had to-we were almost on our last johnny-cake.

20

FEAR

I BID a quiet farewell to our jungle camp and the Singing Creek. Strange how its primitive beauty had grown upon one. . Vines and shrubs and even small trees would probably choke the clearing before we saw it again. With a native guide in the gloomy dawn we slipped away, each carrying a shred of blanket and a johnny-cake. A mile down the creek, we left our own cut track for the native pad. This was the way up which an occasional band of Daintree natives visited those on the Bloomfield side. The route had been used from time immemorial, but only occasionally. The Avengers had used this pad, and our scrub-man had come along it. But on all its climbing, winding course no trace of human beings ever having used it was visible to any but to those with jungle-wise eyes. In those occasional places where sloping terrace corners had stretched out roots like tautened cables, very sharp eyes might notice a smoothness on the pattern across the roots, such as years of bare feet might make on a metal plate when treading in exactly the same place. The plainer sign, however, in these infrequent spots was the thinner carpet of leaves from the trees. Natives, unless civilized "camp" boys, never cut tracks.

Walking in among the trees, with a side-on twist of the shoulder to turn aside the vines, we travelled silently and rapidly, skirting the edge of the creek so that when the undergrowth became too dense, we could push out into the waterway and there walk or hop from boulder to boulder. They were slippery boulders, often covered with a black deposit of vegetation that caused them to glisten as if oiled. The rushing water was ice-cold but we travelled barefooted, as often before. Where boots helped us travel quicker, we wore what remained of them.

Presently, when the creek fell away in falls, we had to leave the bank's walls of creepered rock and cling to the jungle edge, sometimes hanging out over precipices as we reached from tree to tree, sidling along a ledge like crabs fearful of falling into the pounding tumult below.

As we climbed the first downward grade the leading gorge began to form, sharper and deeper, gloomy and black, a humming sound increasing to a roar as additional creeks poured in their waters. Lower down the big creek got rougher and we were forced completely into the jungle, trusting all direction to the native, for there was nothing to guide us except that we were– continually descending.

When gloom was fast darkening to apparent evening there was a brightening amongst the trees ahead and a few minutes later we stepped out into a little forest pocket redolent in the beautiful sunshine of late afternoon, with the smell of green grass and forest trees in flower.

We slung down our swags, gazed up at the sky and breathed in the clear pure air before turning straight back into the scrub. Our blackboy had "spotted" something. His sulky-lipped, unsmiling face almost brightened up every time he located something to eat. Eagerly he led the way back to where a creek trilled over rocky bars under green moss.

The native cut a come-back-quick, cut off the long point and all but the first hook, then tugged off the leaves with savage jerks. Kneeling down in his greased nakedness he bent over a rock slab and thrust the come-back-quick deep within a crack. He probed about with his hooked vine that made little clucking noises in the water in the crack, then dexterously he drew up a fat, bright-eyed brown frog wriggling on the hook. Gripping its webbed foot he brought the frog plop down against a stone, flipped it over his shoulder and went on fishing. It was soon dark, but by that time he had jagged quite a little heap of frogs.

We boiled the billy and hungrily devoured the last johnny-cake. Then the blackboy slung a score of frogs on the coals. They sizzled up quietly and gently, their comical little legs curling up first. They smelt quite appetizing. I turned my frogs on the coals to make sure they were cooked, then nicked the little round ball of intestine out of them. They were delicious, each a soft, tender, juicy mouthful; no bones.

Above our tiny forest pocket was a circle of blue sky with little golden stars. Around us a wall of blackness. A fire-fly floated *out* from the scrub, like 'In emerald that flashed and died.

"I wonder what we're born for?" I mused.

"To live!" answered Charlie.

"But we die!"

"Never!" denied Norman's soft voice. "Death means only the change through which we pass into life again; life in a different body with different senses. Nothing dies actually. After death everything forms again into something finer, something grander. Even the stones can 'die.' Stone is smelted into iron. The iron 'dies' in turn and is smelted into steel. But the original ironstone lives again in that steel. No, death is only a profound change."

Presently Norman drew attention to a ghostly effulgence deep in the jungle: an eerie mist shedding a glow-worm light, that as we walked towards it lit dimly adjacent tree-trunks. As we crept into the scrub towards it the glow became tinged with pink, then brightened into a pillar of pulsing, shimmering light. It was a decayed tree-trunk, alive with some species of vegetable or insect fungus. We could detect the certain life, for the light beat with a ceaseless, tremulous pulsing. And yet that dead trunk appeared decomposed by day.

The next day long before we reached the gorge of the Daintree we could hear the wind blowing and sighing along it like a wind from a distant sea. We walked hungrily, with the biting hunger that grows with rough continuous exertion. We came out on a forest pocket and gazed straight down and along the ruggedly beautiful gorge of the Daintree. Its jungles rose in vast walls of green to open forest ridges crowning the mountain edges.

Far below tumbled the rocky river. A whispering coming from away down there might have been a nation sighing.

The final climb down hundreds of feet to the river, down a rounded wall of red slippery clay, clinging to roots and tufts of grass, was a hazardous job. Once I slipped and rolled, desperately catching a friendly bush that held. Much relieved, we dropped down on to a little shingly beach and gazed up at the broad ribbon of sky.

"What a climb the two runaways must have had," said Norman reminiscently. "And the storm raging too!"

"The gorge must have been howling like the devils in the Pit," answered Charlie.

We walked down the beach, the shingles clattering under our feet, until a precipitous spur jutting straight out into the river barred our way. Fourteen times we had to cross and recross as we wended our way down. We crossed by gripping hands, feeling for a foothold amongst the black slippery boulders. Leaning our weight against the stream as the waters hissed and cried around and past us. When my feet were dragged from under and fingers slipped from Charlie's clutch the native came plunging after me. I remember my billycan bobbing past looked blacker than his face in the spray. The billy went spinning from rock to rock until it was sucked under. The darky clutched my hair and held on with his foot wedged between two boulders until Charlie came. After that, we made the living chain longer: my rescuer advancing, Charlie gripping his outstretched hand while stretching out the rifle to Norman who reached back his arm to me. Thus in the centre of the current it was the rifle and two arms which spanned the dangerous part and gave the leading men more distance and a corresponding chance to get a foothold in steadier waters and hang on while we crossed. So, *too,* while they were crossing Norman and I had a good grip and could, hold the chain should either or both of the others slip or be dragged under. I was increasingly thankful as we worked our way towards the river-mouth. As the river widened the current began to lose strength, and the boulders were not nearly so plentiful.

There was plenty of game in that gorge of the Daintree: pigs everywhere; we saw almost droves of suckers; pigeons hooted across the gorge; again and again we saw the scarlet head of a turkey regarding us from the foliage; and the very first quiet rock pool we came to held fish. They lazily swam to the shallow edge and gazed at us.

Hungrily we pulled some "native dynamite," crushed the leaves between stones and scattered them over the pool. The fish leapt for the leaves to hurriedly dart away. Several minutes later they were swimming in agitated circles and presently came to the surface, struggling desperately to keep their bellies from floating uppermost. Quick and lively we had them on the coals while Charlie shot a sucking-pig, It was a gorgeous meal. We camped there that night.

That native dynamite invariably grows handy to a pool. When crushed and flung into the water its juice possesses the power of blinding, stupefying, sickening, or sending off their equilibrium, any nearby fish. The juice of some varieties turns the water a milky colour, that of others a light brown, while the juice of yet others shows no effect. From the effects of all but a few poisonous varieties, the fish quickly recover if fresh water is flowing into the pool. The roots of some shrubs and the bark of certain trees have a similar effect upon fish. In these juices, possibly, is another anaesthetic for medicine.

We were not to get to the river-mouth without a thrill (I still remember it). Our troubles seemed over. The walking was much easier; no rocky spurs now barred the way of the wider, easier flowing river. Under a fast widening sky the massive heights of Mount Alexander and Peter Bette loomed up to the left; the river was opening out in verdant flats to the right. We were walking in Indian file through cane-grass to our belts along a well-trodden native path, when the tribesman in front hissed warningly and crouched. We crept up and peered over his shoulder. On a clean sandbank across the water lay a fine fat alligator in all his squat ugliness, fast asleep. A willy wagtail cheerily danced and chirruped on his head. Charlie fired. The alligator immediately twisted round and plunged into the water.

We simply stared at the sandbank, the tracks were there but the alligator had gone. So had the willy wagtail. Charlie, who could hit a turkey's head poking from the foliage of a tall tree, missed an alligator in plain view at sixty yards!

Not saying a word, we went on down the path and halted where it entered the water-the last waterhole we had to cross. In it was an alligator, wide awake. It is easy enough to wade an alligator-infested river, but to wade a pool where you know one is waiting, is a different matter altogether.

We sat down for a long time. It may have been one's nerves, possibly the anxiety of the last month and the feverish search for gold on insufficient food; probably it was just sheer fright; but I know if my mates had turned back on the long return trip to China Camp I would have followed without a word. It was the native who ventured first. He was a warrior, and the gamest man of the four.

Every flood alters the bottom of a river-crossing, fills with sand a hole here, scours out a hole there; perhaps shifts the fording place a hundred yards down or upstream, or possibly washes it away altogether. Our volunteer had now to find the ford here.

The bank proved steep. He slid into water waist high, and ventured out slowly, prodding down with his spear-butt, feeling the way with his feet, his mouth tight-lipped, his bloodshot eyes staring down before him. The stream was broad, the current steady. Charlie sat ready with the rifle. Cautiously the warrior probed and felt his way out, worming to right and left as the long spear warned him of deep water to either side. Presently he was up to his neck, poking the spear into a deeper hole in front.

I watched fascinated as he carefully returned and tried again, seeking for the invisible ridge of sand and shingle over which we could cross. Then, standing planted near the centre firmly against the stream, he screwed around his head and nodded. I was in the water right with the Bairds. They are such excellent watermen that I took no chances of being left more than a foot behind.

A man will walk across an alligator-infested river with much more confidence than he will swim. So long as his feet are solidly planted he feels he can put up a fight. He can, if the water is clear, see anything coming too, and kick up a hell of a fuss. And his mates have a much better chance of helping him. But if he is swimming he is helpless, and the alligators know it. They can come at him from behind, from below, from any angle, and he doesn't see them coming. Another thing: the natives say that an alligator, when it sees the legs of a man moving along the bottom, thinks the strange things can see and is afraid to attack.

But this was a dreadful walk across, especially when the icy water came creeping above one's waist, then chest high, gradually laying its icy hand on his throat. One had to stare at the sky to keep the water out of his mouth while he needed all his eyes to watch for that awful snout. At the same time one had to grip for a toehold among the sand and stones. I shall never forget wishing that I could step sixteen feet in one stride. No matter how hard one tries one can wade only very slowly when deep in the water. And the last man is always terrified lest the alligator should snap at his stomach.

But it didn't. We sat on the opposite bank for some time to recover; then thankfully took a wide, grassy flat and walked on down the Daintree.

Around us was the most beautiful land we had yet seen. Grass like lucerne along rich river-flats and brightly foliaged timber. Over the river to the left, the big sombre mountains with bright caps here and there where the sun glinted on forest spurs. The wide quiet river mirroring tree and mountain. We talked about taking up some of this land when we reached civilization; this land "must come." But, of course, as with other chances we had, we did nothing. The first picture-show I saw in Brisbane after my return from the war was a film showing the new sugar settlement on the Daintree.

We stayed at a fine cedar home. Strange to find that house there in the wilds. It was Fischer's place; one of the boys was there looking after cattle. There was a cedar-getter farther down the river. And (another strange thing) a white woman living happily and alone in all that loneliness. A large tribe of blacks also inhabited an area of the river.

The rich lands near the river-mouth had been taken up about twenty years ago by cedar-getters, who, after floating to the sea all the easily accessible logs, endeavoured to turn their holdings to farming purposes. They were years before their time and eventually the entire river was abandoned and went straight back to the wilds.

21

SPIES OF THE COAST

FOR a day or so we lined our insides with civilized food at Fischer's place. The butter, beef, and damper must have livened up our brains. Anyway, we developed a brain-wave, and enthusiastically decided on an investment in Luck. Norman was to return to China Camp with the blackboy, forward our few ounces of gold by the mailman to Cooktown and with the food-stuffs that came in return load up the natives and proceed back to the jungle camp. That gold would buy enough stores to keep him prospecting until Charlie and I could earn and mail some money. While we were cutting cane he might drop on the gold we had been seeking so long. When Charlie and I had "cut out" the season we would return via Cooktown with stores for a more prolonged attempt.

On the shore opposite was the native camp, some hundreds there judging by the beehive-shaped gunyahs among the shrubbery. By the slow smoking fire fronting each visible gunyah squatted groups of men; spear bundles, points upwards, stood against each gun yah entrance;· gins squatted in scattered groups gossiping shrilly as they pounded palm-nuts into flour; dogs lay about in the sun. Odd dawdlers strolled about, some just returning from the hunt. A fishing canoe drifted downstream, the spearman standing ready at the bow. With spear poised and the sun shining on his body, he looked a bronze statue. A young mother came down to the stream, a wooden coolamon filled with pounded nuts upon her head. A toddler followed her, his chubby fists clenching flat pebbles to throw out upon the surface of the water. The mother put down her vessel and knelt by the stream, laughingly warning the toddler to stand well back from the water. He made his first throw and the stone smacked the water, skidded with a chuckling splash to strike and skid again. The toddler raised his arm for a mighty throw and stepped right to the water's edge. One swirling surge and he was grabbed in the jaws of an alligator, his crushed scream moaning out with the terrible cry of the mother. She leaped at the great reptile even as he turned, her screams unending as she thrust her arms at the jaws that locked her child. Following a howling rush of dogs, men snatched their spears and raced, shrieking and yelling, straight down into the water. Hysterical with rage, they plunged out to their waists where the mother, her thumbs in the eyes of the alligator, with the strength of madness kept wrenching his head around to the shore. They swarmed upon him, thrusting with spears, smashing with wommeras, while swimming dogs bit and scratched in a swirl of water. The beast let go of his prey and, spiked with many spears, lashed out and disappeared. Those knocked over struggled to rise while others grasped mother and babe and plunged back to the shore.

As we gazed the death-wail rose – an awful sound. With faces to the skies, and long-drawn wails of anguish, women ran about crying, throwing up their arms, then ran to kneel by the fires and throw ashes upon their heads. Men walked round and round in circles, heads bowed, moaning.

One morning Charlie and I started off, leaving Norman to dawdle a day or two longer. He had a rough trip ahead of him anyway, going up and up. We believed in our hearts he would do no prospecting, that he would wait at the Bloomfield for the stores and lead the lotus life until our return. Anyway, even the gamest natives would not have stayed long with him at the jungle camp.

We expected a thirty-odd mile walk via the river-mouth then along the sea-coast to Port Douglas. There was no track, of course.

Our bank was flat country, well grassed, heavily wooded. In a few miles, however, we got tangled up in the mangroves. It was exceptionally low tide, so we sought short cuts through the water-pools and heavy blue-black mud that surrounded those dwarf trees. Soon we were stepping over and upon their maze of stilted roots. It was quite cool with very few mosquitoes; but the sandflies were snappy. Out in the open somewhere sounded the harsh call of a crane. Every now and again came a decided plop as a long torpedo-shaped seed dropped off to stick in the mud. The rising tide might carry that seed a hundred miles away to start a young mangrove forest on some lonely island shore. We heard whispered gurglings and burblings of queer mud- and shell-fish, with ploppings of air bubbles from the mud where some beastie under below liberated gas while digging out his home. Occasionally one heard the low whistle of some mangrove bird. On umbrella-shaped roots, queer little fat fish were hopping; lively little nuggety brown chaps that hop up the roots and look at you.

"I suppose," said Charlie, as he shied his toes clear of a crab-hole, "if we told the chaps down south there are fish that hop about like a bird and can live out of water, they'd call us liars."

"As mad as spring snakes," I growled.

We plodded on into a sighing rustle, like a dishful of glass beads shaken together, as an army of fightable little soldier crabs scuttled menacingly aside. They sat back on their rumps, brandishing claws energetically; whole armies of them. As we passed they closed up the ranks behind and looked at us. Pity help a lone man should he be stricken helpless in those mud-pits. Gladly we heard the booming of the sea.

A slight break in the mangroves disclosed a circular creek enclosing a mud islet, densely shrouded with mangroves.

"Looks like a moat around a tumbled castle," said Charlie dubiously. "Some old place flattened *out* and overgrown with trees, and the moat slimy with stale water and full of dead men's bones."

"Don't give me the creeps; we've got to cross the dashed place."

"I wonder if that mud is firm!" said Charlie. "Have a look around there and see if you can spot any alligators or sharks. I'll look this way. The water is fairly clear where it's deep."

The creek was already waist-deep; it would be over a man's head at high tide. If we crossed on to the islet, then crossed again, we would keep our straight line. We could hear the sea distinctly now. If we turned aside we must climb roots and plough considerably farther through mud before reaching the beach. We chanced it.

We saw neither alligator nor shark, and the mud on the creek-bottom only sucked us down to a little above the ankles. We went straight on across the islet, twisting our way in between the mangrove trees, to stand in complete surprise.

There was a camp! – invisible until a man was right on it. Just a few trees chopped out in the heart of the thicket. A low, muddied tent, the roof just below the mangrove branches. A rude framework of poles, lashed to the mangroves above the roots, formed a rough floor above the dampness. Inside the tent were lashed two folding bunks with heavy mosquito-nets set over them; some lashed boxes; a kerosene-tin and a primus.

We stared in amazement. A camp there seemed past understanding. Such an eerie place! Such awful loneliness! The high tidal water sucking up through the roots, alligators nosing along in the night, mosquitoes, sandflies, fever! We just gazed at one another.

Charlie guessed almost instantly. I turned out a box. It contained odds and ends: two natty silver-mounted hairbrushes (fancy silver-mounted hairbrushes in a quagmire of the sea!); some stamped envelopes with foreign addresses; a foreign hair-oil; some drawing-pencils and draughtsmen's accessories; and a handful of military cartridges!

We satisfied ourselves; feeling deeply serious, young chaps though we were, at this first-hand evidence of a foreign nation going to such clever lengths to spy the unguarded coast of our country. In such a place, there was not even the chance of a native stumbling upon this hidden camp; he would not have understood it if he had. There would be an innocent fishing lugger by day, of course, away out at sea, mapping its allotted area, too-certain channel ways through the Great Barrier Reef. What this camp was for we could only surmise. Something to do with sounding the river-mouth, we thought; probably with a view to a camp for the concentration of troops, in some future time. If so, the geographical and tactical position had been faultlessly spied out. Opposite, on the northern side, was the uncrossable scrub range. On this bank, was the flat land, quiet, uninhabited, within thirty miles of the commencement of civilization with its cultivated farming lands, its road systems and railway. An army with stores could land and concentrate unseen and unmolested here. When perfectly ready, one night's march would land them at dawn into surprised civilization.

Opposite the tent, across the creek, was a channel leading away towards the river-mouth. We could see the channel winding into gloom where the mangrove roots and branches had been cut to allow . a dinghy access. The men in it would pull themselves along by the roots and branches on either side.

The possibility of those chaps being hauled out of bunk by a prowling alligator at night was what got me most.

"Not at all!" said Charlie. "They'd be working at night in the dinghy away out in the river-mouth, or somewhere just outside up or down the coast. The lugger would come in during the night and shift them about as required. Come away lively out of this. If they are anywhere handy and return, they'll settle us. Not a soul would know."

I grabbed a handful of evidence and we hurried away. In due course, I posted my little curios to the Naval authorities and promptly received acknowledgment. By then, of course, the birds had flown.

With greatly relieved minds we emerged from the mangroves on to clean white sands pounded by a welcoming sea. Bright sunlight and a cool breeze, with sea-plover running along the beach. In excellent spirits we walked the coast; it was a promenade to us. We only had three shillings in that pocket of Charlie's which did not have a hole in it, but our hearts were overflowing with the joy of life. Whistling along the coast, whooping at the sand-snipes that ran in shrill alarm before us, we walked over a beach where a fortnight later lay a little fortune. A dead Chinaman, with two hundred tins of opium rolled neatly in his swag. Each tin was worth £11. If Charlie and I had only dawdled!

But we didn't. We crossed several black, nasty looking creeks instead, haunts of the alligator and opium smuggler. We saw neither, and camped that night at the hut of a German who was pioneering a little coconut plantation.

Next day we bowled along into Port Douglas, a cheerful little spot noted for its one-armed wharf-lumpers and sugar-loading records. Here we had a shave. We had not noticed the necessity until the stare of the inhabitants put us wise. The toes were out of our boots, the seats out of our strides, but we didn't notice any of these things until the waitress at the pub whispered: "Come and see the two wild men from Borneo!"

Without a penny in our pockets we walked inland to Mossman, a bright little sugar town. The township was crowded with flannelled men, men in shirtsleeves, brown-limbed men in "Jacky Howes." In the main street a policeman was having a rough and tumble with a young Italian cane-cutter. The frolicsome immigrant was roaring our pet Australian word in Italian. But the policeman flung him in the dust and knelt on him.

There was a strike on! This was desperate news for Charlie and me. In the sheerest of forlorn hopes I inquired at the Post Office. Yes! There was a letter for "I. L. Idriess." It was a £10 cheque from the *Bulletin* for "pars." We were made. We went straight across to the pub and bought long beers and a big meal. Then a pair of strides, a shirt, and boots for each, tobacco, and a sugar-bag of tucker. After that the twenty-mile walk over the range to Mount Molloy.

We found Mount Molloy to be a closed-down copper-mine, a good-hearted butcher, a dozen houses, a timber mill, and a handful of the finest chaps in the world. Middlemiss kept the two pubs then, Frank Crowley the butcher's shop, Johnstone the timber mill, Jack & Newell the store.

Old "Tommy the Chinaman" was one of the characters of the township. He was the shrewdest billiard player from Mount Carbine to Mareeba, he could pot the red with the surety of a hen laying eggs.

Molloy was fairly lively at week-ends when the timber-getters came rolling in with their big logs and a few of the station men and tin scratchers from round about turned up. But it was a happy sort of liveliness; every man would rather do his neighbour a good turn than a bad one.

The boys told us that there was a "bit of tin up on Mount Fraser, about six miles out." They pointed vaguely across the trees to where the mountains began. "Used to be a rich creek up there once," they explained. "But there's no one there now only an old hatter as mad as a snake."

So we bought a few more provisions to carry on with, and halved the weight. Charlie halved his share and putting each half into a sugar-bag, tied the ends together. I did likewise, and slung the double sausage across my shoulder. One weight thus balances the other. A load is much easier carried that way.

Whistling cheerily and shouting a farewell to Old Tommy we set off down the road and soon turned off on to the pad. The way was through forest country. The pad was faint, only perceptible here and there. It had been made by the bare feet of the old hatter on his periodical visits to the township.

"He must be a quaint old bird," I remarked as we steadily climbed a grassy spur.

"Yes," replied Charlie, just ahead, "you'll like him by all accounts; they say he's a 'wild man.' The police talked about taking him away and sending him to an old men's home for safety. But the township said that would break his heart. So they let him be."

When almost to the summit, we found one half the mountain top to be forest, the other half scrub. We rigged a rough camp in the open forest, but within sixty yards of the scrub edge. We felt all bucked up with the "newness" of the country and the camp. Charlie was whistling. He always liked the mountains.

"There's plenty of space to breathe up here," I remarked.

"Yes," he answered, as he cleaned the frying-pan with a fistful of grass, "it's open here right enough. A man will sleep like a top; and when he feels like a walk-about the mountains up that valley look inviting. Hullo!" he added, "What's this coming?"

I looked up to see the most quizzical face in the mountains. It only had one good eye, all screwed up at that, which set off a crinkly smile in a sheaf of gingery whiskers. He was bald on top too, but grew side manes of ribald hair poking out over his ears. He looked like chuckling, and he chuckled. A gaunt figure, his bones stood out in his patched flannel and pants. The pants were made of bags. He stood on surprisingly large bare feet with knuckle-bones standing out like marbles; the toenails were lumps of horn. He spoke with a dreamy drawl and a chuckle in his voice. He introduced himself as George Stewart.

"'Old George,' they call me." He smiled and added that he was "real interested in company."

"Are you mad?" he chuckled.

"Well," answered Charlie doubtfully, "not that we're aware of."

"People don't know everything," confided the hermit with a meaning wink. "We lives an' learns. Anyways, the people down below in the township say I'm mad, livin' all alone up here with the snakes. I bet you boys don't stay here more'n a week."

He peered at us with a queerly anxious expression.

"You're on, George me lad!" accepted Charlie with certainty. "We stay right here until we get enough tin to take us away again. That means we want a ton, for we travel far when we go."

The old man's smile faded noticeably; his lined old face looked almost tired. He picked up a straw and chewed it, his one eye wandering around our stores as if gauging the limit of our staying capacity. He waited a while, squatting there on his haunches, joining in desultory conversation as we finalized camp, then climbed back up the hill crown with the setting of the sun.

"Nice old man," remarked Charlie, as we watched the stooped old figure climbing away. "If he is an example of the bush, then he's enough to drive a man back to the city."

"He's got an eye like a hawk," I smiled. "He missed nothing."

"By Jove he didn't! That eye of his took in everything. But if he thinks he's going to scare us away with yarns about snakes, he's met the wrong men. I wonder what he's nursing up here, a hoard of sovereigns of a skeleton in the cupboard?"

"Heaven knows. Fancy a man living for years in this wind-blown loneliness. It's a wonder the wind at night doesn't drive him mad."

"He is mad!" declared Charlie. "Look out, there's the billy boiling!"

We got quickly to work on our new venture. The "tin creek" was only a hundred yards in through the scrub. Its banks were mounds of greenery where the scrub had grown over the piles of forking stones thrown out in the old days. But we prospected, got promising results, and saw that by sluicing we could make a good thing out of "old" ground that had been worked before. Water was the difficulty. We were almost on the mountain summit, hence there was the barest trickle coming in from the heads of ravines. But jungle work puts a man wise to the ways of water. We blocked water that was running away underground in the creek-head, built a dam, and in a fortnight were sluicing merrily, getting a clear run of four hours water a day, with handsome results. In no time we won and sold a couple of bags and were on good terms with the storekeeper.

The old hatter used to noiselessly appear and inspect our method of work. We would look up from our job to see him staring down at us. He declared no good would come of our toil, it was "too damn modern."

"Youse boys ought to be satisfied with the dish, shovel, an' pick; not try an' wash the whole bloomin' mountain away. You'll get more tin if you take it easy."

"So will my aunt," replied Charlie as he set the water rushing down the race. And added as we watched the old man stooping back through the scrub, "He's got a dead set against us. He wants to drive us away. I wonder what for?"

"Perhaps he has a young wife hidden up there." "The woman who would marry him," said Charlie emphatically, "would make love to a hairy baboon."

I picked up the sluice fork and the prongs tinkled as they bit in under the loose stones. A scrub-bird whistled joyously from a tree above. I laughed at Charlie. He was rather a nasty chap if set against a man near his own age; but for old age or helplessness he would go to any lengths to give a man a hand. He bent over his work and scowled as I whistled to the tinkling of the forking stones.

In the evenings after sunset we would sprawl out in the glorious air beside the just glowing fire. Evening used to settle down in a sort of pale blue that gradually darkened. In the hush that always comes before the night voices start whispering, Charlie would murmur:

"Old Wire-whiskers is decorating that bloodwood again!"

And I would know the old hatter was peering at us from behind a big tree a little above our camp. His own camp was up there somewhere.

22

THE OLD HATTER

DURING that first month on Mount Fraser, we thought the old man was spying on us from some unfriendly motive: Not so. He was terrified that we were "murderers," who would shoot his birds and kill his goannas and furry bush friends. In later times (we revisited Mount Fraser after this story ends) I came to realize with what apprehension he had watched our every move. He had actually crawled night after night to the back of the tent, listening to hear if we were planning "to kill things." Only when he was sure that we were not ruthless killers did he take us to his warm old heart.

We accepted his first gracious invitation to "come up home," and climbed through the tangled grasses up a knoll overlooking our camp. Throughout the years, his bare feet had worn a pad like a wallaby pad from his hut to the main track which led down below to town. Our expectant curiosity was fully realized. Below a forest gum that towered from the forest edge out over the scrub, a granite boulder the size of a house leaned shakily, half in the forest, half in the scrub. The forest side of the cold grey stone formed the back of the hut, the thick line of scrub trees was a living wall, the other wall and roof a grotesque patchwork of saplings, bark sheets, flattened tins, bags, and palm thatch. Four sheets of mud-bound bark made the chimney. Luxuriant grass on the forest side grew up the sapling wall and thus bound it, while from the trees forming the scrub wall, vines and creepers reached out over the other side with riotous tendrils meeting the upgrowing grass. The vines were in flower. Their pretty mass of pink and white hid the patchy simplicity of the roof, adding a quaint dignity to the dozen cheeky little birds that hopped among the petals.

On hearing our voices, a big grey goanna, handsome with yellow spots, waddled out from the low, open doorway. His snake-like head was raised high above a hefty chest and fat stubby forelegs as he stood and surveyed us.

"That's 'Spots,' " introduced the old hatter with a half apologetic, half anxious smile. "He comes loafin' around lookin' for a feed. Get ter hell outer this," he added sharply to the goanna. "Go on! Get outer this!" The goanna ignored the order; it twisted its long neck and regarded us sideways from a bright, suspicious eye. It poked out a long tongue and dubiously licked its snout. This disdainful action caused the old hatter to move instantly forward. "' So did the goanna, dodging the hatter's foot to a nicety as it slithered into the grass. It scurried to a huge burnt *out* stump, twisted round by a hollow root to hiss witheringly, then waddled into its burrow, taking its time and dignity.

"There's no harm in him really," smiled the old man's one eye. "He'll take to yer when he gets used to yer ways."

With a lordly air he invited us inside. A musty, earthy old place, smelling of bare rock, dank scrub, and sweet grassy forest. The rudest of bag bunks was propped by forked sticks along the forest side of the hut. Seeds were dropping from the grass-stems that had poked through the walls. A wild lilac creeper was in full bloom half within, half outside the hut. Steel drills had been hammered into the rock, forming supports for shelves holding a medley of tins and bottles. A few smoke-blackened boxes comprised the furniture. There was a rude fireplace of stone and clay, with a blackened billycan slowly steaming, suspended from a chain. On the stone hob squatted a monstrous green frog, regarding us unblinkingly.

"'Greenie,'" nodded the old man. "He hops in from the scrub now an' then."

"Don't snakes come in too?" I asked.

"Oh they don't do no harm – not to them who knows their ways. An' Greenie can look after himself."

Several lizards clung to the forest posts on the sunny side of the hut, their eyes like tiny black beads as their lively heads craned towards our coming.

"Take a seat," offered the old man affably. "Squat down anywheres at all. Make yourselves at home; don't take any notice of the blokes in the hut."

"The lizards!" I smiled.

"Yes," he twinkled, "a porcerpine calls sometimes at night, so you'll have to watch where you sit when you come visitin' after dark. An' if you're barefooted, look out comin' up the pad. I planted me foot on his quills once an' they nearly stuck into me. You see, the blokes come visitin' from all ways, the scrub fellows from the scrub, the forest from the forest. They feel safe that way an' they can each dive back into scrub or forest if they has ter leave in a hurry. They clash, sometimes."

For the first time, Charlie laughed. I laughed.

The old man rocked back and forward until tears streamed from his wrinkled eye down into those riotous whiskers. We were friends.

"Who is boss of the roost?" I inquired.

"Me!" he replied with dignity, "though Spots thinks *he* is. Sometimes when a strange snake comes crawlin' in there's the devil to pay. Spots goes for him tooth an' claw, jealous I s'pose. If the snake's a big feller Spots backs his carcass in between me feet an' fights from there so as I've got to take. a hand if things gets too willin'. I've seen some ding-dong goes in this little house."

"Don't you ever get bitten?" asked Charlie. "Sometimes. But that's nothin'. It's only happened three times since I've been on the mountain. Snakes don't try to harm me; they know I won't hurt 'em. An' besides even if they do bite there's herbs in the scrub will cure any bite under the sun – if you knows where to look for 'em. The only bite I don't like is fleas; they're that sudden on a bloke with a tender skin."

I glanced at his "skin," it was really blotched hide from exposure to many suns while the soles of his feet must have been fully a quarter-inch thick. He had not worn boots for twenty years. He put the billy on, all on tenterhooks to play the host.

"A drink o' tea is better'n a pot o' beer any day," he chuckled, "'specially when you haven't got the beer."

"I don't touch it myself," said Charlie, non-committally.

"Neither do I. It rots yer insides away."

We glanced at one another as he threw a handful of what looked like dried vine leaves in the billy as it came to the boil. He poured out a panni kin full of watery looking fluid and handed it to me with a flourish, filling a milk-tin for Charlie and a treacle-tin for himself.

"Have a taste!" he invited and drank, smiling at us with his old eye twinkling over the tin.

The steam of the concoction smelt like Charlie's face looked when he sipped it.

"Don't yer like it?"

"No."

"It's not bad," I broke in. "What is it?"

"Herbs. I makes all my own tea outer herbs that grow in the scrub. They're healthier an' tastier."

"They are *that!*" agreed Charlie.

The old chap's eyes fairly sparkled as he apologized for his rough home. He loved it. He hung on our words of approval.

"Any night," he invited eagerly, "come up an' have a yarn. Don't wait ter be arsked!"

"What about that porcupine?" inquired Charlie doubtfully.

"I'll kick him out if I remembers," promised the old chap heartily. "I'll know you're comin', becos his quills sticks up when he hears anyone."

"What if he's curled up outside on the pad in the dark!"

"Wear yer boots, boys. Old pore won't hurt you but you might tread on a death-adder. Sometimes they lie out in the pad at night."

We liked our new locality, but only as a change. We were too near civilization. About six miles below our mountain was tiny Mount Molloy, connected by a little puffing railway over the flat country to Biboohra, then

Mareeba on the Cairns-Herberton line. Towards the coast, twenty odd miles away, was "the Mossman" and Port Douglas. On the inland side of the range, were cattle stations; then twenty miles farther along, the isolated but busy wolfram camp, Mount Carbine. A lively little place that was, crowded with what the Yanks call he-men. Our Mount Fraser marked a break in the range. From its summit, looking south, we could see a vista of flat country and hills right to the big Cairns range. But Mount Fraser was really the start of "our mountains;" the first mountain from which a continuation of the main chain ran far up north to our jungle camp, then on towards the Rossville chain and the branch chain towards Mount Windsor. Around the foothills of the range on this Fraser end, on alluvial· flats mostly, "Cockies" were making a struggling appearance. I suppose and hope they are well established now. They were fine men and women. But up where we were, there were only "two young coves and an old hatter," with a medley of snakes, an occasional wild pig, a lot of minor things of the wild, and birds.

The cockatoos were a riotous crowd, simply bubbling over with bird happiness and the urge to tell all the world about it. They followed the leader unhesitatingly whether he wished to fly or settle for a yarn; to roost or fly far over the range seeking grass-seed. They displayed fine team work, if noisy. In late afternoon, like a white cloud they would come flapping heavily over the dark green valley below, to rise up the mountain and settle in a noisy flock on the big tree above the hatter's camp. The massed birds made those branches look like a gigantic snow cauliflower picturesquely leaning out over the dark green scrub. I shall never forget the first evening of our mutual acquaintance. Charlie and I were enjoying an early tea when the birds arrived. A voice screeched "George! George!" to the accompaniment of screeches, raised crests, and other not so well pronounced calls of "Garge! Garge! "

As we stared up at the knoll a hidden voice distinctly yelled: "George! George! How are you, you – old hatter!"

"George! George!" screeched the birds to a craning of necks and ruffled crests.

"What do you think of that!" exclaimed Charlie in a dazed sort of way.

"He must have taught the birds," I answered. But he hadn't. He chuckled next morning as he explained that it was a tame cockatoo.

"Musta gone wild an' flown in with the scrubbers. The first mornin' I woke up an' heard 'George! George!' yelling over the camp, I was dead scared. Just lay there thinkin' someone had come for me. Couldn't recognize the voice at all an' knew there wasn't a soul on the mountain but me. When they flew away out over the valley he was still screechin' 'George! George!' an' me gazin' away out acrost there as if I'd seen a ghost. But that evenin' when he come back with the mob I yelled 'George!' an' he screeched back

'George! George!' like as if he was home agen. Since then we've both taught the mob quite a lot. The young coves is comin' on fine. If I lives long enough I'll have the best trained mob o' talkin' cockatoos in the Commonwealth!"

"Do the dashed things screech in the morning?" asked Charlie dubiously.

"Oh yes! But you'll soon get used to 'em."

Charlie looked black. He hated being awakened early.

Sometimes in the dead of night we would be awakened by frantic screeches calling on "George! George! Garge! Garge!" and Charlie would turn over and swear all the more when we heard the old man yelling from outside his hut.

"George! George! What the hell are yer wakin' me for? A man carn't git a wink er sleep with you noisy blighters! Mob the cat! Sink yer beaks inter him! Ain't there enough of yer! Expect me to come climbin' up the tree in me shirt do yer?"

Charlie would swear and cover his head with the blanket. I'd listen while gradually the birds quietened and George retired grumbling to his hut. When that prowling native cat disturbed the birds, they were not slow in calling on their old friend under below.

At dawn after a noisy medley of "talk," screeching, and quarrelling the flock would fly off down the valley to their breakfast of grass-seeds along the distant forest spurs.

We put all our energies into tin-getting. Under our present circumstances, being so close to civilization, we did not have the delay of hunting for food. It only meant a day's walk down to and from the township to carry up a decent supply. And Frank Crowley, the butcher, overcame that loss of time, for he sent a boy along with packhorses and a month's supply of tucker right to the camp. Our relaxation was the campfire talk at night. Old George was a source of never-ending interest-to me at any rate.

After he came to trust us, George frequently asked us up to see his claim. We were curious. We knew it must be rich for he seldom worked, and then by methods childishly absurd. Instead of running a stream of water through a long sluice-box and shovelling in the washdirt, he used to kneel by a puddle-hole and wash his dirt in a little battered old frying-pan. A schoolboy could have put through more dirt.

One day we visited his "workings," pushing through tangled scrub almost to the peak of the summit in search of his hidden ravine. The ground here had never been worked, perhaps because there was no running water to work it. Wondering where the old man could be, we at last espied a big black hole under a tangled mass of rocks. It looked more like the entrance to an animal's den than a tunnel made by man.

On hands and knees Charlie crawled in first. We listened. Presently, far away, like the beak of a bird against a tree, we heard a faint tap, tap, tap. We crawled on into complete darkness, then lit matches and went on, twisting like dingoes down that narrow passage among the rocks. But dingoes have eyes that see in the dark, whereas we had hands and heads and knees that could feel. What a sight those faint gleams of match-light allowed us to imagine! Shapes of black boulders glistening with clamminess, gripped by roots like slimy black snakes, guessed-at hollows where the old hatter had gouged out the washdirt leaving the rocks poised one upon another. They "felt" even more than looked as if ready to come crashing down at any moment. We saw at once why his claim was so rich. The only washdirt in it was that sandwiched in between the rocks in crushed layers, and it, of course, was mostly concentrated tin. We were deep down within the bed of what had been a rushing river in ages past. Our sun was a few million years younger when he had shone on that young river. And now, here was insect man scratching in darkness, uncovering the buried secrets of aeons past.

We felt our way farther in, feeling mud under our knees and hands, the match-flares shining in Charlie's eyes as he stared dubiously at the "roof" before advancing crawl by crawl. Those slow, un hurried pick-strokes sounded a little nearer and at last in the inky blackness ahead a faint glow showed. It reminded me of fungus in the jungle at night. As we crawled on, the tapping sounded rhythmic and distinct to the scratching of the pick. We saw the candle-flame then, illuminating the bright outer Binge of whiskers, the dull sheen on a nearly bald head, the bare back and nobby bones of the hunched up old man. He was sitting on the shovel blade: it should have felt icy cold for the seat was worn out of his working strides.

"George!" called Charlie softly.

The bald head turned in utter fright, his mouth half open, his one eye staring wildly, sweat gleaming on brow and chest.

"It's us, George," called Charlie, "Jack and I."

"Oh," he whispered, "I – I thought it was – it was someone else."

23

QUAINT COMPANIONS

As a change from hard work, Charlie and I would take a day's walk along the range summit. There is nothing that rejuvenates a man for physical toil so much, as mental relaxation among beautiful surroundings. To stand on a forest peak and gaze north at mountain-tops alternately uniformed in dark green scrub and sunlit forest fading into distant haze, was a memorable sight. The denser green that sank deep down among them, were the valleys. Charlie used to gaze longingly to where sky and peaks met. Somewhere beyond the horizon there was the Bloomfield, his country. I loved the mountains; the deep life that I know is in them seemed to call to me.

We would sit down, so absorbed at times that we hardly troubled to smoke. We would discuss a trip right up through those mountains. Start from here, with a trusty team of horses and twelve months' tucker; find and follow leading spurs; cut a track through the scrub areas from forest pocket to forest pocket; form a base in each, and prospect an area of country from it; and so on right up to and past the jungle camp itself.

Dreams! The undertaking would have only cost a couple of hundred pounds for equipment and provisions, but Fate declared against it.

The towering kauri-pines, rising in their pink-tinted splendour on mountain slope and in the valleys, excited our admiration. Someday, we were certain, those superb trees would be of great value. We talked of taking up a timber concession. In a few years, when valleys around Mount Fraser comparatively easy of access were cut out of timber, we would be rich men. Why, we would take up concessions from here to the Daintree. The coastal timber we could haul to steamers and the inland timber to the Mount Molloy railway and from there rail to Cairns. There was something in this new idea of motor-power haulage too, a day would come when some form of a motor-tractor would be invented that could climb in through the bush and haul logs from now inaccessible localities. We prided ourselves that we were a bit shrewd.

Dreams again! And yet, a few years later, after the war, the first things I saw at Molloy station were horse and bullock-teams and motor-tractors hauling in the pine from those very valleys.

Man is not the only killer of trees. There is a strangler, which, springing from one tiny seed, will slowly crush the life out of a forest giant. And a bird – a sweet-voiced bird – brings strangler and its victim together.

A species of fig-tree is the killer. A bird unknowingly drops a seed of the fig into the fork of a stately tree. The seed germinates and lowers aerial roots. These develop into encircling arms that reach the earth, take root and swell into living cables that clasp the trunk closer and tighter. This growing octopus drains the life-blood of the tree. Gradually its leaves lose their fresh glory; the sheen upon its bark turns dull; its branches no longer wave freely to the wind; it begins to die; then dies fighting to the last. Only a huge skeleton of what was once a tree is left. There are other stranglers, and vampires of the vegetable world, in those scrubs.

On sociable evenings, we would look up from the campfire at a chuckling – "What ho, boys! What's th' noos?" as Old George came down the pad on his bare feet.

Sometimes the goanna trailed after him at a respectful distance, like a dog none too sure of its welcome at the strangers' camp. George would settle himself comfortably by the fire, squatting with his old face smiling over his knees.

"Why don't you box your tin?" asked Charlie one night, "instead of washing it in that old frying-pan. You'd clean up a ton instead of a few pounds."

"Because I've got sense," George answered defiantly, "While that tin stays in the ground, it's a bank to me. I draw on it whenever I want tucker. If I worked it out I'd have to go and scratch for another claim."

"But don't *you* want to make a wad?" inquired Charlie. "Don't *you* want to see the cities, and life, and other things."

"No," answered George soberly. "There's so many things to see here; the earth an' the sky an' the stars, the scrub an' the forest; things in the ground an' the water; things in the grass; things that go sighin' past in the air at night. What would I see in a city? Shops an' houses an' trams an' people. They'd think I was mad!" And he chuckled as he lit his pipe with a live coal.

"Take youse boys for instance. You're workin' your insides *out* to get a ton o' tin. When you get it you'll go away an' spend it a dashed side quicker than you earned it. Then you'll have to go an' do it all over again. What for? Ain't life short enough as it is, without makin' a livin' misery of each day! The world is goin' to larst for ever but you boys ain't! You'll be dead long before my age just becos you worked yourselves out. What for?"

"Oh well," replied Charlie, "we'll all be dead in a hundred years anyway."

"'Course we will, so why not live each day easy as it comes. You never see the sun rushin' acrost the sky like a mad motor-car tryin' to make up time. If he did he'd die, clean wore out. No, the sun takes it easy, an' he gets there every time."

"But he's got a long time to do it in," answered Charlie, "and he doesn't need things to eat either."

"How do you know?" Charlie laughed.

"You win, George."

"'Course I do. I reckon a man's mad who rushes about tryin' to make money to pay for an early funeral."

He was a queer old card, full of kindly thought for anything that lives. He would have made a wonderful husband for some girl if only she had caught him young. But then, he would have been of no interest to me. Now, he was a being who counted, a real mate to all the funny little wild things of the bush. They seemed to understand him. With queerly modulated hissings he could coax a snake from out the scrub on to forest grass. According to different species he would vary his hissing to the slow, seductive movements of his hands and feet as his one eye stared at the snake. The big carpet-snake that camped in the hut was almost a part of him. He would look at it, twitch his eye, and the thing would glide along the humpy floor, climb over his knee and slowly drape itself around his neck, its big, flat head motionlessly resting on the coils upon his shoulder. The snake knew perfectly well it was not to eat Brownie the rat nor Greenie the frog. All the pets preserved a perfect, though armed neutrality while in the hut, the only boisterousness being caused by Spots the goanna who really seemed to think he owned the show. I've seen him in his greed and jealousy scatter the birds, chase the rat, send the frog hopping and threaten the snake with show of teeth, lashing of tail, and violent hissings. The big snake would lie motionless, steadily regarding the would-be bully out of cold, glassy eyes until George kicked the spotted disturbance out of the hut. Never without a shindy, however. Spots would even threaten George himself, which roused the old chap to a temper of shouts and kicks. But in his heart I believe he loved the beast just a little more than the rest.

Lizards would climb all over him. I've seen three little sun-baskers at one time with their tiny claws clinging to his whiskers while they twisted around to peer at me. His bald head was a trap – for March-flies. He would sit still for an hour at a time to give the lizards a chance. They just loved March-flies.

Birds never feared him, a host of the little beggars made his home their rendezvous. I've gone into the hut at meal-time and there was a bird perched on his shoulder, another perking upon his head, half a dozen chattering and fighting over his bare feet for crumbs. He was always afraid of leaving tea in his billycan when he left camp for work. One evening he had returned to find a little humming-bird drowned in the half-filled billy. The old chap nearly cried when in a low voice he told us about it. And the tragedy had happened several years ago.

The first evening I visited Old George I was not too sure of my reception.

These real hatters are queer coves.

"Wear your boots anyway," warned Charlie. "He'll have all the snakes in the scrub about the place."

To my surprise, on approaching the hut I heard voices. Visitors? Light shone from a chink in the walls. I hesitated; there seemed to be a row on.

"A man oughter knock yer!" came the old hatter's angry voice. "If yer had ther guts to stand up to it I'd do it too yer greedy guzzler. Eat a man outer house an' home an' then insult him! Now just take that 'biff!' an' that 'bang!' an' that 'biff!'" I jumped sky-high as the huge goanna scuttled between my legs going for the lick of his life. With beating heart I heard him hissing angrily in the darkness.

"An' if yer comes back I'll skin yer alive!" yelled the hatter from the hut. Angry mutterings. The creak of a box told he was settling down again. "I'll show yer who's the chucker-out," he mumbled. "An' I'll liven youse coves up too. You're gettin' as cheeky as those young coves down the hill. Company ain't none too good for youse!"

With a rather guilty smile I sneaked forward and peered through the chink. Old George was a dear old chap and I make no apology. He was sitting by the fire, his gingery whiskers looking quite frisky in the light. He chuckled, then chuckled again:

"Diddled you that time, Brownie," he remarked to the plump, furry bush rat which, stretching energetically on its hind-legs was pawing at a lump of damper crust that swayed from a piece of string. Though he leapt, and leapt high he just could not grasp that elusive crust, aggravatingly swinging like a pendulum. Greenie, the big fat frog, solemnly watched proceedings from the warm hearth. A sleek little lizard who should have been in bed, stood looking up with his wee front claws comically gripping the hatter's big toe. Then Brownie used his head, perhaps he had been caught that way before for nimbly he climbed a post and came along a rafter directly above the string. There was a tiny "click" as his sharp little teeth snapped on the string. The hatter roared laughing at the rat's disgust – the string was wound around wire. Cautiously the rat began climbing down the swaying strand, his perky nose held well out in front. He had nearly reached the crust when the hatter held a firestick below it. The rat stood it awhile, turning his head this way and that from the coiling wisp of smoke. Then he leapt to the earthern floor, rubbed his eyes with little forepaws and stood directly under the crust, squinting up. A shrill cry from the big tree above startled me too. The rat's ears pricked and twitched like those of a listening wallaby, the frog's solemn eyes grew brighter. The old hatter wagged his head at his apprehensive friends.

"Hear him, Brownie," he warned. "That's our night-hawk, an' he's a-lookin' for you. Ain't you glad you're livin' with me in a nice, cosy hut, eatin' damper an' sugar instead of bein' out in the cold scrub with the night-hawk eatin' you. But it's time to go ter roost. Here's yer supper."

He cut down the crust, then stroked the eating rat kindly. It was a pretty rat, its rich brown fur showed a rosy wave to the firelight. Greenie flopped heavily from the hearth for his share of the caress while the lizard nibbled at the crust beside the rat.

I sneaked down the path a bit, started whistling, and walked up to the hut again as George called cheerily:

"Come right in boy an' we'll have a billy o' tea."

24

HAPPY DAYS

CHARLIE and I needed no alarm-clock. At the greying of dawn the cockatoos on the hatter's tree above would lift frowsy beaks from beneath their wings and proceed to tell the world about it. A few querulous, complaining squawks at first, just to wake the mob up, then with the brightening of the east all hands would awaken the whole mountain side. Two hundred cockatoos, crests rampant, greeting a new day! Their competitive yells, squawks, and screeches would go ringing down the mountain side and off over the misty valley to be answered faintly but distinctly from unseen compatriots miles away. Then would come shrieks of "George!" "George!" "George!" "George!" "Garge!" "Garge!" while they stretched their necks and wings, preened themselves, picked a beakful or two of bark and did a short walk-about on the limbs.

Charlie would roll over in bunk, gritting his teeth, as a lazy yell faintly answered, "George! George! You-old hatter! Wake up, you lazy cow! "

"And go frazzling to hell!" exclaimed Charlie as he leapt out of bunk to light the fire.

He could seldom go to sleep again if awakened early. He would stand swearing as the birds in a screeching white cloud flew down from the tree and, with a parting chorus as they swooped low over the tent, sped like dazzling snowballs away out over the valley.

We toiled hard to make the most of the water we had before the dry season completely drained the springs. We were doing fairly well and indications were that we might strike a "patch" at any time. A patch would mean £100 worth or more of tin in a couple of weeks; in which event we could sail back to Cooktown, *en route* to the jungle camp, loaded with provisions for twelve months.

As a mark of great esteem, old George showed me how he mesmerized snakes. It was a remarkable exhibition in which he used his feet, towards the end. He showed me too on occasion how he made friends of birds and hopping things. He had an extensive knowledge of plant-life too, so far as that particular area of scrub and forest country was concerned. He knew where to seek edible nuts, roots, and bulbs, and above all how to prepare them.

"How do you know whether new bulbs you find are poisonous or not?" I asked.

"That's easy," he chuckled. "You eat 'em!" One bright morning, his funny old face squinted down over the creek-bank. He never wore a hat but always his smile.

"Drop the pick an' come along, Jack," he chuckled mysteriously. "I've got somethin' good to eat."

"He'll poison you sure!" warned Charlie. The old hatter chuckled hugely.

"When Charlie's survived all the belly-aches I have," he grimaced, "he'll know a lot about plants."

Charlie sniffed, and went on with his work. He was levering at a boulder that had fallen from the bank above and blocked the tail-race. I gave him a hand to roll it out of the way then downed tools and followed the old chap a considerable distance along what he called a pad; the vines grew so profusely that they were looping round our necks most of the way. Presently the old man halted, peering at the ground. "Go on! git out of it!" he ordered. Rather mystified, I peeped down among the vines and there, its thick heavy coils camouflaged among the leaves, was an almost greyish looking snake, right at his bare feet. "Git out of it!" ordered George again. The snake never moved, its eyes stared stonily up. George lost his temper. He lifted back his foot and caught the snake a resounding thwack upon its thick-set coils. As the surprised reptile uncoiled, the hatter got in another kick that landed the wriggler well clear of the pad.

"You've got to let these coves feel whose boss at times," he growled. "That cove seems to think he owns the whole damn mountain lately."

A bit farther along, among a medley of rotted logs, the old chap pointed to a shaving of bark curled up under a ledge of rock.

"See where that bark is pokin' up like as if a big mushroom was underneath? Well, just shift that bark."

I did so and uncovered a pretty scar let thing as large as a man's fist, pineapple shaped. It grew up from a stalk that was deep in the decayed loam. It had no leaves.

"They've died out," explained George. "Anyways, you'd never see them; they're broad leaves, a sort of pretty dull red. They grows quite flat under the dead leaves from the tree. They dies before the fruit comes anyway. That is the fruit. Taste it."

He showed me how to peel it; it had a thick, juicy yellow skin.

"The skin looks nice to eat but it burns hell outer yer mouth. I nearly went mad the first time I tried, couldn't close my mouth for three days."

The flesh inside was a pulpy pink and yellow. It was delicious, with a fragrance that made me long for more.

"It's just lovely, George," I said, and his old eye laughed to my esteem. "Are there any more?" He shook his head.

"They're very scarce; don't come every season. I think the rains has something to do with it. They don't like too much rain an' they don't like too little. The heat o' the leaves must be just right too or they won't come. There might be lots more about but you've got no chance of findin' 'em. The only sign is when the fallen leaves poke up, an' they're liable to poke up at any sort of plant growin' up underneath. But they're worth findin', puts pep into a man, makes him feel he's young an' ticklish."

"It does so," I smiled. "I don't feel like going back to work with this pleasant tingling feeling inside."

"Don't!" advised George. "There's plenty more days comin'. Come for a walk instead. We might find some new snakes."

George found the snakes all right-under rocks and logs, coiled around roots and looped upon the branches of trees. He found them out in the open forest, coiled upon the warm granite rock and on a grass tussock like a jewelled turban round the head of an eastern potentate. They were of all colours and sizes, from the sightless little thing that burrows under the soft loam to the ten-foot carpet-snake basking in the sunlight.

One would never have dreamed that so many snakes were to be found on such a limited area. But then one would have passed over and beside and under them without seeing them. A man in the jungle and forest sees but few of the things that see him.

Telling Charlie about it that evening he merely replied:

"Old George is a bit 'snakey' himself."

"How do you mean?" I asked.

"Oh, there are a few men who have an affinity tor snakes. Seem to understand them, and the snakes respond somehow or other. I know a native who can squat down and whistle a snake to him from hundreds of yards away, especially if, like now, it is the snake season. He can lure quite a crowd round him, can tie them in knots. They take it as if the touch of his hands mesmerized them. He handles them in a peculiar way. If you let him touch your wrist just after he's been handling one, you would feel as if a snake were coiling round your wrist and creeping up your arm. You can feel it in your blood: if you shut your eyes you'd see the thing. I'll introduce you to that buck next trip we make north. Old George is not so expert by a long way; but he is 'snakey' all the same."

"How about that plant he found?"

"It's a new one to me. It might grow farther up north, the jungle is big enough. It sounds something like the 'secret plant' of the natives. But their plant is a fungus growth. Only the old men are allowed to eat it. It is supposed to restore youth."

Years later, I heard vaguely of this secret plant from tribe after tribe all the way up the Peninsula. But, as with other "sacred secrets," they kept its secret well.

When our stores ran out, Charlie and I would go whistling down to the township, camp a night at the pub, and carry back a light load of provisions the following day.

The town had known lively days when the rich copper-mine was working.

Old Tommy was a "white-man Chinaman," one of those coloured characters fairly often met with in a far-out township. His was a merry old laugh, with the high-pitched Chinese twang that grew very excited when he was "potting the red." I have already referred to his skill at billiards. He would challenge any stranger, commercial man, wandering parson, timber man, or prospector, and become so delighted at each win that it was all the vanquished could do to keep him from "shouting" out of his turn. But he was a good-hearted old chap. He never forgot a friend. That is a splendid trait in the Chinese character; they will never forget a man who does them a favour.

Many a good feed of bananas I've had at old Tommy's place; fruit was very welcome after the hard tack at Mount Fraser. All Tommy's fruit had to come from Cairns, up the Cairns range, then along the little branch line to Molloy. His little house was down past the pub, towards Rifle Creek. The rough slab walls of the somewhat smellful abode were decorated with dried lizards, fish, snakes, birds' claws, smoked hearts and livers and things.

Tommy had a set grievance against Old George. He loved him and indulged in a regal jag with him on the rare occasions when the hatter came to town. Never once did they intend to do it, but they used to end up by trying to outdo one another – the hatter drinking rum, old Tommy whisky. Their never-settled argument was as to who fell asleep first. This news was somewhat of a shock to us.

"So he's human after all!" exclaimed. Charlie.

Old Tommy's face immediately lengthened into the serious expression of a man defending a friend.

"But the poor old man must have some relief boys. You can't expect him to live all alone up on that lonely mountain and have no happiness when he comes to town. He'd go mad!" defended Tommy in spirited English.

"He seems a bit that way no matter where he is," smiled Charlie, "judging by all accounts."

Old Tommy looked shocked: his lower lip had a habit of drooping down.

"Don't you believe it, boys," he said seriously. "Old George is a gentleman when he's in town. Pays his debts at the store and butcher's. Not over quarrelsome. Pays for his liquor in his turn, and takes it like a man!"

We laughed at Tommy's reproachful eyes. But Tommy had another grievance against his gentleman pal besides the rum-whisky one. He complained bitterly that though his friend "Old George," who could bring him all the galls in the bush if he liked, would not bring him one single goanna gall!

Tommy used to dry the galls, and frogs and livers, hearts and tongues and similar innards, and claws of birds too, for medicine which he sold to compatriots in Cairns and on the Atherton Tableland.

We could easily imagine that Tommy had far more hope of getting George tipsy than of getting him to kill a goanna for its gall or anything else!

The white people of Molloy township were some of the nicest I have ever known. Life would have to last longer than memory for me ever to forget them.

We were always ready to rush the billy on when we reached camp, while I would hurry up to the old hatter with his delicacy of fresh bread and meat. On one such return from Molloy I heard the usual argument proceeding and knew that Spots was in disgrace again. An "argument" was always comedy to me, so I just tiptoed stealthily along.

"You lazy guzzling loafer, livin' on a man with never a 'thank 'ee' in return! Ain't I told you a dozen times the stores ain't come yet! Ain't I told you the boys ain't arrived? Do you take me for a liar? Ain't I told you we're out o' meat a week? Do you take me for a bullick station? Keep yer claws out o' me feet or I'll land you one in the ribs!"

The old hatter grumbled away while I smiled in my heart. The usual little birds were chirruping on the bushes that blocked the never-closed doorway, some were hopping in and out of the hut. On the earthen floor at his feet was the big goanna, its sharp cut head darting out as the old man feigned to throw it a morsel. He laughed uproariously at the reptile's beady-eyed discomfiture. But I knew he was eagerly listening for my arrival, far more so for his pets' sake than his own.

"Thought you had it that time didn't yer, Spots? Well never think you've got a thing till you've got it. Not that you ever earns it. You're gettin' that fat you can hardly crawl. An' remember this, you spotted loafer; I was watchin' you this mornin' when you was watchin' that little blue fantail buildin' on that honeysuckle there. If you pinches any of that bird's babies I'll boil you alive in fat, you hound!"

A big March-fly went humming in through the open door. The sleek little brown lizard by the fireplace darted his head around to locate the noise. The insect hovered a moment then settled on the old man's big toe. It selected its position, put its head down and its tail up and commenced boring. The hatter was stroking the head of the goanna. It must have been a full minute before he felt that something was amiss. Now a March-fly carries a boring apparatus with a sharp sting and though the hatter's toe was leathery he soon opened wide his one eye. His mouth screwed up at the corner; he lifted his foot, gently cocking the toe straight up. Instantly the lizard darted forward, its little head thrust out and the big fly was gone where it would do most good. The hatter's pent-up feelings burst:

"Why the flamin' blazes wasn't you quicker?" he yelled. "Couldn't you see the damned fly eatin' me toe off! Blast yer ! You're gettin' your inside too well lined, that's what you are. You're that darned lazy you oughter live with a hemperor, you ought."

Rubbing his toe and grumbling he sprang up in delight as I entered the hut to a flurry of little birds.

"Here's your bread, George, and a few pounds of fresh beef. Frank Crowley is sending all our bulky stores up to-morrow by packhorse."

"Good boy, Jack! Come right in. Here's where we eats again!"

And Old George received his stores with open arms.

Norman Baird, Charlie's brother, 1915.

25

THE FIGHT

WHEN feeling like a change, Charlie and I would spend the week-end down in Molloy. There we gained in vigour by mixing with our fellow men. We learned, too, lots of little things from strangers who were living distantly around us but engaged in pursuits quite different from our own.

As a rule, the little crowd would begin to roll up on Saturday afternoon; timber-getters freshly shaved in the luxury of a clean white shirt; lanky cattlemen in corduroys and leggings; a teamster or two from the dusty Carbine road. Perhaps a bush commercial traveller; certainly a few "tin-scratchers," and maybe a "scheelite-chaser" with a wandering gold prospector to give colour to the discussion on minerals. There would always be a bush nomad or two-those chaps who float along the far out bush-tracks doing goodness knows what. The little paddocks close by and the open bush around would be dotted with horses more or less hostile to one another, while saddles adorned the stockyard rails or were stacked carefully along the veranda.

Cattle-dogs and tykes of lesser degree roamed the street as if they owned it. These high tailed roysterers were the envy of those superior dogs compelled to stay by their masters or trained to remain out on the flat guarding the master's horse. Charlie and I used to patronize the big pub until a pretty bush waitress came to the one across the road.

With the exception of the inevitable irrepressibles, the boys seldom drank to excess. We met more as a social gathering. Numbers of these men saw only their own mates for weeks and months at a time. During that period they toiled hard, living on beef and damper. A man can live for a very long time under such conditions, but a mental and physical change does him the world of good. The feed and yarns awaiting the traveller at either of the Molloy pubs were well worth the long rides of those who came to enjoy them.

The Sunday morning after Charlie sold our first output of tin was glorious; bright sunshine, the smell of flowering trees, and all around us the quiet Sunday of a very small bush township. Chaps sitting on the low-built back veranda smoking and yarning. Another group on the woodheap smoking and yarning. Others like big lazy crows perched on the fence rails smoking and yarning. Clatter of dishes and girls' high-pitched voices coming from behind us in the kitchen. A whiff of stale beer as the brawny-armed publican wobbled along the veranda and out across the yard carrying a drooping basket of dead marines. Some wag whistled the funeral march, so that all might know he had once visited the Cairns pictures. Sharp and clear came the hoof-beats of a galloping horse followed by a cloud of dust as the local tomboy showed her paces. Her little dress lifting in the breeze and her strides for all to see she flew past the stockyard fence and away down the slope to a rousing cheer from the lads.

Fat hens clucked importantly around the kitchen door, keeping an eye on pullets that were foraging suspiciously close to the handsome black rooster. That Romeo lifted high his head and crowed with might and hauteur. A brown dignitary answered with a burst of defiance, ruffing his feathers before he resumed pecking. The black rooster glared across the yard, blew out his chest and gave it another go, more prolonged, more raucous this time. At his full height, he stood glaring and awaited results. He got them. The brown rooster walked straight in amongst the pullets!

In a moment feathers were flying as the rivals got fairly into it. How the gravel flew! It was a battle royal: we shouted the dogs off and enjoyed the set-to until the girls ran out and spoiled it with a dish-cloth. They were indignant girls; they accused us of "setting the roosters on!"

"You can't *set* a rooster," replied a youth scathingly, "anyways hens won't lay eggs unless roosters fight. It eggs 'em on."

The crowd laughed and the girls retired remarking they couldn't see anything to laugh at.

From the milking shed the pub cat walked majestically across the yard, *en route* to the kitchen. A tyke lowered his head and charged. The cat lowered his tail and marathoned into the kitchen with the dog at its heels. We roared at falling dishes, shrieks, hubbub, and barking as dogs from all across the yard flew into the chase.

Of course, it brought a more indignant reprimand from the girls. They emerged in a body wiping the spilt milk and potato peelings from their aprons. There was no use denying it; they had actually seen us "sool" the dog on. As a matter of fact the dog had taken the matter into his own hands, or feet.

When things quietened down again we were treated to a host of dog yarns. Even the ambitious chaps lolling at the kitchen window drifted towards the more interesting conversation, to the chagrin of the girls. There were grave stories of wonderful cattle-dogs, horse-dogs, camp-dogs, kangaroo-dogs, possum-dogs, cattle thieves' dogs, and just plain "dawgs."

Charlie and I glanced at one another. We could have told some tales here. Tales of pig-dogs, of dogs that save men's lives.

I don't know whether the tykes around the yard understood they were the subject of conversation, but at the psychological moment, as if to emphasize their importance, they started fighting. A fox-terrier began hostilities by snapping at some mongrel's leg and it took strong men to settle the resultant melee. But it started all over again, for dogs came flying from everywhere to join in a howling mix-up right across the yard to avalanche down along the veranda and into the kitchen once more. Then there was hell to pay while a wiry whiskered old chap who did not own a dog, was dancing upon his hat yelling:

"Let 'em at it! Let 'em at it! Let the best tyke win!"

But the owners of prized dogs braved the wrath in the kitchen and pulled and kicked the snarling tangles apart.

"Could 'av' been the best fight I've seen in twelve months!" regretted wire-whiskers. "Why didn't you let 'em at it?"

"Why don't you cut your throat?" snarled a cattleman whose dog was limping on three legs.

What the girls said was mostly in hysterics.

When peace had been forcibly restored and the girls quietened somewhat, keen argument broke out, for several men present owned a dog that could fight "anything with hair on!" The dogs each imagined he was the terror boasted of for he glared from the leash of his master's knees at the tykes who had been shooed away but were returning and snarling remarks as they squatted on their haunches just out of stone's throw. Licking their chops while showing their teeth, they growled humiliating things to the dogs that were not allowed to leave their master's presence. It was plain that a renewal of hostilities could be expected at less than no notice.

Someone suggested a "bob in!" So we all trooped across the veranda into the bar and draped ourselves across it. It was a cool drink, in a long cool place with shut doors. Of course, the dice rattled again to another bob-in, while every man's companion started to tell a dog-story. The last story had not been started when the dinner-bell rang.

After a jolly dinner in bare sleeves we trooped out into the shade fully content at expecting a lazy afternoon. Not so. Darby MacNamara and his brother came along at a flying gallop to wheel a dozen frisky colts into the yard. Mongrels ran forward barking but trained dogs stood prick-eared, expecting something doing. "Any of *you* coves like to try your hand at something fresh?" laughed Darby. No one answered anything in particular but the stockmen present were delighted. . What better holiday than in breaking-in a horse!

We strolled across to the yard, draped ourselves critically across the rails, and surveyed the wild-eyed youngsters. They snorted, bustling around one another in shivering alarm. One lively young chestnut lashed out at the rails.

"They're a bit fresh!" drawled a lean cattleman.

"Not bad sorts!" remarked another critically.

"Give 'em a go!" advised wire-whiskers eagerly. "You coves can ride anything with hair on."

"You're wanting to see someone's neck broke, as usual," smiled a burly timber man.

"No such luck! I've been comin' to this pub three year now an' I've seen only one man killed."

"Come out to the timber camps then, an' you'll see some more."

"Oh what's a log fallin' on a man! I want somethin' exciting."

"Well, go across an' hit the policeman on the jaw!"

"He's gone out into the back country chasin' them cattle-duffers."

"Well hop into this yard then and bite that chestnut on the leg."

But the man who wanted to see a man killed declined.

Two of the colts gave us worthy exhibitions, from pig-rooting they rose to heights of bucking that were beautiful to watch-from the rails. I was glad I was not on their hunched, twisting backs. You could hear the riders' teeth rattle as the colts jarred straight down on four hooves to rear in a desperate attempt to throw themselves backwards. Only two riders were thrown flying in the dust to the delight of wire-whiskers but-no one was killed. It was late afternoon when the last colt had had his first grim taste of man. They were a dusty, sweaty, subdued lot of young horses that trotted out of the yard to Darby's command.

Someone suggested a bob in!

It was a long cool drink, everybody enjoyed it while discussing the recent riding. Of course, at the second bob-in everyone was telling of wonder horses he knew, horses that bucked the saddle off as well as the mall, "fair bucked out of their hides, as a matter of fact!" Then it started. Just a quiet argument; it wasn't much to fight about; but it started over a dog. Wars have been fought over less, so they say.

We filed out into the yard again full of pleasureable anticipation, old wire-whiskers in delight. This was going to be the end of a perfect day.

The combatants set about the job methodically, each a little distance apart stripping off his flannel surrounded by his immediate friends. They were both big chaps, six-footers, solid men with brawny chests brown as their muscled arms, hard and tough from open-air living and solid toil. The square-faced chap was a timber-getter; the other a gouger from Wolfram Camp, his lean jaw set and stern. We formed a ring, kicked the dogs out of the way, then the two beauties faced one another and got into it with bare knuckles. The fight was staged in three-minute rounds and skin and blood were flying in the first three minutes.

It takes a good man to come up to it again after each three minutes of slogging. Fighting is the hardest work known to man. After taking a few punches where they hurt most, he feels just like nothing on earth. Though pride forces him to rise on his feet to take more, he feels like going home to mother. Looking on is another matter altogether. These two chaps were determined to win; each could give and take hard blows; each had plenty of wind. That's where it hurts most – "in the wind."

You could hear those thumps well across the yard while the tough bare knuckles to the side of the head smacked like hammer blows. I was glad I was stopping none of them. After each three minutes, the sweating men sat on a box and filled their lungs while their seconds fanned them, rinsing their mouths out with water. Then at "Time" they jumped up and walked straight into one another again, hard faced, savage looking, breathing deep and heavily. They grunted when they struck and the man struck grunted too, you could hear him catch his breath. At the fourth round you couldn't see the colour of their faces or chests for gore. As slowly they grew tired they began to hug one another like bears, swaying as one strained to throw the other in between the punches, gasping as they snarled into one another's eyes, their muscles all bunched up, their mouths open now, their faces with the starey look of men whose minds are forcing the exhausted body to still stand up to it. They fought for exactly half an hour before a hazily aimed blow brought the loser to his knees, the winner's knees all groggy as he panted waiting for the fallen man to rise.

A four-minute fight is quite enough for me. But then I'm no glutton.

The tea-bell rang, loud and clamorously. The girls had been looking at the fight, craning their necks from boxes on the veranda. We all trooped into the bar for an appetizer. Tea could wait.

On that particular week-end we did not start out for Molloy until after lunch on Monday; and it was already dark when we climbed up to camp. As we walked up over the last little rise we saw the fire blazing brightly, the billy on, while a hunched up old chap with red whiskers sat staring down the track, a big goanna staring beside him.

"Hello! Hello!" he yelled, "I was just comin' to look for you. What the hell yer been doin'?"

"Settin' Molloy on fire?"

"No, George," answered Charlie, as he dropped the bag of provisions, "it's chaps like you do that. Look out that dashed goanna doesn't scoff your fresh meat!"

As George made a furious swipe Spots plunged out of reach.

"Of all ther damn cheek!" the old man roared. "Git back to your camp. Go on, git!"

"He likes his meat raw," said Charlie, as the hissing goanna backed away into the grass.

"He'll get something else directly," promised George threateningly. "Now tell us all the noos," he asked eagerly, while dropping a chunk of steak into the frying-pan. "Sit down an' spell; I'll cook yer tea. Everything in the camp is lovely; I've been lookin' after things."

"Good-oh," said Charlie thankfully. "I was half thinking that flaming goanna of yours might have been clawing around."

"No he ain't," vouched the old hatter grimly. "I've kept an eye on him. Give him a belt in the ribs if he comes down here annoyin' you coves agen."

Charlie grunted. I smiled, remembering Charlie's oft-repeated attempts to get near enough to give that goanna "a belt in the ribs."

I sat by the fire regaling George with the news while Charlie unfastened the tent-flap and looked over our things inside. We heard him rummaging for the tucker-tools, then he lit the hurricane lamp – and yelled.

"What the blazes is the matter?" I shouted.

"A death-adder! – in my blankets. I'd turned the blanket down too in the dark! "

We looked into the tent. There was a nice fat death-adder all right, two feet long, lying snugly on Char lie's bunk.

"I'd rather have Spots in bed with me than him," mused old George.

"I'll have neither!" answered Charlie savagely, as he seized a pickhandle.

Old George was quite cut up that he had missed the fun in town. "Nothin' happens when I'm in," he complained, "let alone a fight."

"Not by all accounts!" agreed Charlie, as he threw the dead death-adder on the fire. "They tell us the last time you were in town you tried to fight the policeman!"

A huge smile overspread George's face.

"Go on! They told you that now!" he insinuated.

"They did. And they told us it took three men to pull you off!"

"I might have done something," said George amiably, "if the cows had only let me at him. I wouldn't hurt the policeman mind; he's one of the whitest men I've ever met."

"What did you try to pull him to pieces for, then?"

"Oh, that was the rum, not me. There orter be a law against rum."

But old George would not stay after he had cooked our tea; he was thinking of his waiting pets. He took his share of fresh meat and bread and toiled slowly up to his camp, Spots wobbling along behind.

26

THE HATTER'S HOLIDAY

CHARLIE and I continued winning a little tin, but we would have won it in highly paying quantities had the water not been drying up fast. For sluice work you must command a supply of water. And to make ground pay that has been worked before, you must sluice-almost always anyway. Our little dam depended for water solely on mountain springs. A peculiarity of these and similar springs, we noticed, was that the water flowed more freely in the morning, dying off noticeably towards the afternoon. During the small hours was apparently the best flow of all. Why, I do not know. Perhaps the moon or the pull of the earth has something to do with it. Bush-lore advances a number of theories.

As you may not know anything about "tin-scratching," here is what Charlie and I were doing. We were winning alluvial tin, otherwise "stream" tin. In appearance it is very much like coarse black sand. It collects mostly in watercourses, having been washed there from mountains during ages past. The tin sands lie generally on the bottom of a granite or slate creek, mixed up with washdirt, boulders, and gravels. To get rid of this surplus overburden as quickly as possible man brings along running water to help him. He cuts "races" down which the water rushes carrying with it the debris. The tin sands, being very heavy, sink to the bottom of a "tail" race, out of which it is later "cleaned up."

Now that our water was petering out it was no longer possible for us to work the ground with pick and shovel and make it pay. We needed water. The wet season was soon due. Given running water, if only for two months in the year, and an hydraulic plant, we knew we could win more than enough tin to pay for the other ten months' prospecting for gold up north in the jungle. It was an alluring prospect, two months' work per year down here, then freedom from monetary troubles while prospecting our gold country.

But we wanted another £100 to buy the necessary plant. It looked a poser. Then I had a brainwave; my old Dad! I hadn't written home for years, but thought if I sent a wire for £100 it might be answered. It was worth trying.

So we decided to cut the preparatory races then send the wire in time to make the plant before the wet. An hydraulic plant on a small scale is easily made, and it will do a far greater amount of work than men can do sluicing by hand. We could buy the iron in Cairns, have the pipes made in Mareeba, rail them to Molloy, then transport them with Dick's horses up to our claim on Mount Fraser.

We decided to bring my old mate Dick Welch into it. Dick was a Cooktown lad, and we had heard in a roundabout way that he and his old horses were "spelling" in Cooktown. These horses would be the transport for the pipes from the township up to the claim, and for the tin down to the township.

"After the races are cut," said Charlie one evening, "you'll be able to land in Cooktown just a few days before Mee-lele's wedding."

"Yes, I think I'll go down. I promised her you know, and the people would take it badly if I was actually in Cooktown and did not look them up. How about you coming too? After all, it will be a break."

"No. I'll get busy on the shed. We'll only just have time to get the plant all set up before the wet is due. You won't have much time on your hands either."

"If Dick is in Cooktown, he'll have the horses out in some handy paddock. He can be attending to the stores while I slip down to the Bloomfield. I wonder what Norman is doing?"

"Any need to ask?" yawned Charlie. "Hullo, here comes Old George. One of these nights he'll plant those big bare hooves of his on a death-adder. I killed another on the track yesterday morning."

But George only chuckled when we warned him. Seating himself comfortably by the fire, he reached for a coal for his pipe.

"Why should I worry," he puffed, "I'd die quick! I've had a long spin and I'd rather go out sudden."

We silently hoped the old man's wish would be realized. If he took ill or met with an accident all alone up here on that mountain his end would be a lingering one.

Coming from work one afternoon we heard the old familiar grunt and on tiptoeing through the scrub saw a wild sow (an infrequent visitor here) in a noisy state of excitement plunging through the bushes to wheel around the trees chasing a twisting, turning, writhing carpet-snake. I had rarely seen any snake, let alone a carpet, move so fast before. But this chap was too slow. The sow plunged her fore-hooves on him and tore him to pieces despite his frantic bites, her squealings hurrying a troop of suckers to the feast. They made quick work of the fragments, squealing and squabbling over the squirming pieces in tugs of war. Charlie sped away for the rifle, and that night we enjoyed roast sucking-pig.

That was one of the quiet nights. They come often in the bush; we just lay by the fire and dreamed. It is so easy to smoke and look into the lazy flames and just let thoughts, and intuitions, longings, and phantasies come. It is the atmosphere, I suppose. A man is so far away from everything; there is no hurry, no desperate worry as to what tomorrow may bring forth.

This night Mee-lele came. Her pretty little face seemed dancing in the flames; her presence felt so near at last that Charlie had to speak three times.

"Old George's coppers are hot."

"Oh."

"Yes. He's going into Molloy tomorrow: can't hang out any longer. Got any mail?"

"No. Blow the mail."

"Oh Mee-lele, Mee-lele," hummed Charlie, "lil-y of beau-ty, flow'r of the scrub!"

"Yes," I sighed, "too nice a flower for old Assan."

"Watch the Killer of Pigs," advised Charlie soberly. "He is dangerous."

With a cheerful "So long, boys," old George trooped down the mountain track next morning, wearing clean patched khaki strides with the legs rolled up showing his bare feet to advantage. With his pipe alight and an empty sugar-bag over his shoulder, he went happily on his three-monthly jaunt, promising faithfully to be back by nightfall.

When the old chap had not returned on the third night, Charlie sat by the fire listening anxiously. He did not even throw a stick towards the rustle in the grass where Spots was waiting too.

"Something might have happened to the old man," muttered Charlie for the tenth time. "He should have been here last night."

"He thinks nothing of a night," I replied from the tent. "They're all the same to him."

"Up here, yes, but not down in Molloy. He'd be worrying all the time about those lizards and birds of his."

"Ye-s, but he only goes down once in four months or so. When he gets a drop of rum in he's sure to forget the menagerie for a night or two. The wonder is he is not stark staring mad, living up here all alone. But he's all right; he knows this mountain in the dark."

"Not with rum aboard. He may fall down any of those gullies. It's a black night, too. He's half blind and he's got to feel the track with his feet."

"The old chap will turn up," I replied confidently as I yawned comfortably in bunk. "He may die in that tunnel of his sure enough, but not out in the open and half full of rum. Besides, they won't let him come to harm down there."

A little later Charlie came into the tent and took the hurricane lamp, his brown face frowning as he turned up the light. I shammed sleep and heard him walking away down the mountain path. Three hours later he woke me up as he growled his way into bunk.

"I've been right to the foot of the mountain," he swore. "The old devil's not there. I'm going right into Molloy to-morrow and I'll drag him home by those whiskers of his."

I had got nicely to sleep only to leap awake at a frightful yell: "What is it?" I gasped as Charlie and I bumped heads.

"I don't--"

Again that startling yell, wild howls of laughter. "Jack! Charlie! Wake up, youse lazy jackasses! George! George! Garge! Garge! "

"It's him," breathed Charlie. "I'd like to break his neck!"

So felt I. We lit the hurricane lamp as the old hatter peered in at the tent, his one eye fairly dancing, his whiskers all over the place, his face a hundred wrinkles as he laughed in wonderful humour.

"What-ho!" he yelled. "Here's to the merry widder. What-ho! What-ho! What-ho!"

"Been having a good time, George," remarked Charlie as he pushed past the inebriate and fanned up the fire.

"Wow! Wow! Wow!" yelled George as he followed us on groggy feet. He slung the tuckerbag starwards, waved his arms and yelled "Wow! Wow! Wow!"

We laughed, he was too comical with his smile and his ginger whiskers at all angles; he had left for Molloy with his whiskers so nicely combed too – with our comb.

He sat down with a thump right on Spots whose busy head was in the tucker-bag. To an immediate upheaval of hatter and lashing tail, the goanna scuttled in violent hissings back to the grass.

"Leave him alone," laughed Charlie, "he's been waiting for you these two days past. Here, get some of this tea into you, it will do you good."

The old man's trembling hand seized the pannikin, "Look in the tucker-bag, boys, there's the remains of a bottle there. Have a drink."

We did so, and at daylight helped him back up to his camp. He was asleep when he hit the bunk. We could never have got rid of him otherwise.

"Thank heaven that doesn't happen often," breathed Charlie, as we walked back down the track. "The old devil will be seeing all the snakes and goannas in the world now."

From the big old tree high above, the cockatoos were screeching, "George! George! Garge! Garge!" as the sun arose big and golden red.

In the afternoon, I went up and peeped in at the old hatter, and was well cheeked as the favoured little birds scurried out of the hut. The old man was dead to the world, a hopelessly "dead" look on his leathery old face. Spots was there, his big length sprawled across the floor, his beady eyes ever watching. Brownie and Greenie were there too, while a bright-eyed little lizard basked on the old man's forehead. It was better to let him sleep it off.

He made a hell of a row that night, though. Cunningly he had hidden another bottle before he reached our camp. He kicked all his friends out of the hut, hammered a kerosene-tin and "sang" and yelled half the night through. He was a week recovering.

A few nights later Charlie said:

"Well, the race is just about finished. When do you start for Cooktown?"

"The next boat from Cairns."

"Mee-lele's wedding is drawing pretty close."

"Yes. Have you changed your mind?"

"No jolly fear. I've just about got over my little romance and I don't want to wake it up. I'll get busy with that shed, then start the trellis work over the creek."

"Right-oh!" I agreed.

Gossip among the mia-mias.

27

THE GREEN-EYED DOG

SO we sold all the tin on hand and Charlie saw me off in the little Molloy train, via Biboohra to Cairns. The trip was great; wearing new clothes, staying at hotels, sitting down to meals already cooked, money to pay for it and all, a man felt as independent as a king. Then from Cairns by the weekly steamer to Cooktown. Another pleasant change. No pushing through scrub or swamp or climbing rocky hills; just watching the coast and dreaming, almost too lazy to smoke. I had walked every mile of that beautiful coastline. How its beauty appealed to one from a deck chair! How imposing was the hazy bulk of Peter Botte when viewed from the sea! What a quaint little thrill it gave one to know that one knew all about those stone Sisters, and the Amazon Gins on Alexander, while every other passenger gazed, wondering what were the names of those apparently inaccessible fastnesses. What was the country like? What lay farther in among the mountains? Were there any white men there? Any natives?

Considerably later, while well out at sea and still steaming north, we passed the Bloomfield; and those passengers did not even know we had passed a river-mouth, let alone a settlement in behind there. They did not even dream of a Mee-lele!

Cooktown is a bonny town, very pretty with its little white Signal Station upon the hill by the sea. From here the steamer would turn south again, for there are no people, except prospectors and a few cattle-men and sandalwood-getters, farther north in all those three hundred miles until you reach Thursday Island. Cooktown had been my headquarters for prospecting expeditions extending over a number of years. I had come to love its hospitable people, always welcoming the stranger, ever ready with the helping hand for their own people in trouble.

Dick Welch was waiting at the wharf to greet me: his horses were spelling a few miles out. That evening we made our few arrangements. Dick would attend to the outfit and get the tucker packed ready for travelling before I returned from the Bloomfield. I would be away only a week, as the date for Mee-lele's wedding was almost due. On my return we would take the packhorses by the long but only known horse-track around the mountain chain and back past Mount Carbine right down into Molloy.

I left for the Bloomfield per horse with the mailman on his fortnightly trip, going through the outlying tin-fields, then over Mount Romeo on the beautiful eighty-mile track to Wyalla plain and so down to the dreaming river.

The settlement was in a state of great expectation over Assan's wedding. Busy stripping of the gardens for the feast; heaps of manioc, sugar-cane, papaws, sweet-buks, bananas, five-fingers, sour-sops; cases of southern fruit shipped from Cooktown; the storeroom filled with flour, currants, tea, sugar, and all the rest of it.

Pigs were fattened ready for the killing, and a whole steer ready dressed had just arrived from the Landing. Some women were chatteringly busy at the kop-maori ovens, the scooped-out earth steaming as they put in the red-hot stones and laid over them the cool green banana leaves, and the sucking-pig well wrapped in more broad leaves spiced with the ginger-plant on top of that, then covered all with more hot stones, ashes, and earth. There were quite a number of ovens roasting pig and fowl, duck and beef, and quantities of vegetables and fish.

Other women were busy making puddings and cakes; gaily excited over their new dresses, and gossiping of past weddings while whispering of weddings to be. Luana was doing no cooking at all. She was *too* busy titivating her attractive hair. Her rounded arm was prettily dimpled as she combed those tresses with a polished tortoise-shell comb given by the stranger sea boy who gazed adoringly at her. The men, lolling about in clean khaki pants and singlet on the veranda and under the mango-trees, smoked cigarettes and smiled supercilious smiles while quite keyed up themselves. Discreetly they chiacked Assan and he answered good-humouredly, with that pleasantly harsh smile of his. In a wrinkled, preoccupied way he was busy with his clothes; he rarely wore anything but a pair of khaki strides. He had washed his legs and feet too, for a wedding-day carried its social obligations.

Mee-lele was the gayest of the gay, the heroine of the hour; flitting here, there and everywhere; superintending arrangements for the feast; answering merrily and with wit the sly digs of her women friends, and with sharp-edged repartee the pleasantries of the men. Already in a new dress, her raven hair tantalizingly scented, her black eyes smiling brightly, she hurried everywhere on tireless feet. She would be a lovely bride. I was only a youngster, but even so, could not help wondering what she would look like, say, in five years' time, when that fatal colour must inevitably darken the youthful cream of her skin.

The people welcomed me uproariously, the news spread like wildfire that "Jacky" had come. Men, women, and children crowded around. I knew instinctively that the white lad's presence brought spice to the excitement. Assan welcomed me with his small calculating eyes and wry smile.

"Welcome to my wedding, Jack; I expected you would come."

"What greater pleasure than to see an old friend happily married. I wish you luck, Assan." And I really meant it.

Mee-lele's excited welcome revived slumbering feelings. I wanted a quiet word with her for the last time just to wish her luck; and gradually felt piqued at her laughing avoidance. In a boyish way it hurt to be turned down when so full of good wishes. But when taking a sulky stroll down through the banana patch that evening two warm arms encircled me from behind and a warm cheek was pressed to my neck, and all the sulkiness vanished.

Her face grew white and serious as I turned around, her eyes spoke from the heart in silence as we gazed. Then she smiled and just touched my cheek.

"It is all planned, Jacky," she whispered excitedly.

"All ready unless – unless you do what the people expect you might do." She drew close, staring in a questioning, searching way. Then she smiled gaily and slipping aside hurried back to the house, leaving me staring with thoughts that were not too kind of myself.

The surprise she spoke of was past understanding. Something was going to happen to-morrow night and the uncertainty was not conducive to sleep.

The wedding-night came. A dark night, the sky was almost purplish black; Wyalla plain must have been a mat of blackness. A land breeze was blowing down the river, rustling in the banana groves; the leaves sighed eerily. How vegetation responds to the varying moods of the night! And how those moods affect human beings! Mee-lele had picked this moonless night to get married, and Assan had good-humouredly allowed her her choice. So long as he got married, was all that bothered him. But why Mee-lele had not chosen one of the quid, moonlit nights that are so beautiful on the Bloomfield, was a mystery. And she just loved the moon!

Assan's bungalow house was the centre of an elusive excitement as well as of merriment. Assan's wedding was a .great event, long waited for with always the speculation as to whether it would ever take place. In hours only, now, he was to be married. Violins, concertinas, and mandolins accompanied chorused songs sweetly blown away by the wind; lanterns hung from the veranda and under the mango-trees where food for surplus guests was laid. At a look from Mee-lele I strolled from the guests and dawdled down into the banana grove. Through the banana-trees the house and the big low limbs of the mango-trees appeared as if hung with titanic fire-flies as the hurricane lamps gleamed and dimmed and gleamed again. A little figure in white and pink came quickly through the banana groves, straight to my arms.

"Oh Jacky, quick," she whispered urgently. "Make up your mind quick. Run away with me. I have planned everything, everything! In three minutes we can be safe and away."

I hesitated fateful seconds-then looked down at the snarling muzzle of Assan's green-eyed dog. A second later and Assan was beside us, his eyes blazing like the dog's, his very hair on end. He leaped back for the house, the dog behind him. Mee-lele thrust me away frantically, a changed Mee-lele.

"Run, Jacky, run for your life! He's going amok!"

She sped straight towards the river as screams broke from the house; shouts of men, overturned chairs, stampede of people in an awful hurry to get away. I sped after Mee-lele through the garden, over the cleared ground and saw her dive straight into the river. Rowlocks clicked sharply to a low quick whistle. An energetic bundle in shadowy white was dragged aboard as an oarsman slewed around to a gurgle of oars. I heard his deep-chested grunts as he fairly lifted the dinghy out into the stream. To the creak of an anchor-chain unseen workers slaved at a winch; pulley blocks rattled; a sail was hoisted; water gurgled as a craft like a shadow slipped away.

Mee-lele was gone! Her Filipino had crept into the river-mouth with the coming of night and waited close inshore!

Back towards the house excited voices were distantly scattering, shouting warnings of the whereabouts of Assan with his kris. Luana's voice was screaming:

"Run, Jacky, run!"

I whipped out a revolver and ran, afraid of a green-eyed dog-I almost smashed into Ratara as he leapt wildly from behind a palm.

"Go for your life, Jacky! Get a start before he puts the dog on your tracks!"

He grabbed me by the arm, half running away from the house.

"But the people, Ratara! If anyone is killed because of me! I'd better fight it out!"

He waved his rifle and laughed, hastening me away.

"No one is hurt: we were expecting it: we all knew something would happen. Go for your life, Jacky; he will be after you and that will take him from us!"

He gave me a good-bye push and I ran straight for Wyalla plain, seeking to cut the mailman's pad. To have gone up the river to the Landing would have meant being trapped in Assan's own country. The one chance of escape was instant action on the short fifty-mile track straight back to Cooktown. A rifle-shot rang out behind, then another; the sharp ringing echoes told they were from the river-bank. Were they trying to shoot Assan or was he firing towards the escaping cutter? He could not possibly see it, but then a man running amok chops or shoots at anything. When a Malay goes so all hands treat him as a mad dog, for there is no hope of arguing with a madman. If he had raced down to the river it meant a chance for me now fleeing across the plain, and it would take his mind off the people and give all a chance to escape. He instantly would think I had fled up the river to the Landing. If only he would think so until daylight! Racing through the bush with a mind racing too I prayed fervently that Assan would not sink his kris into any innocent person. It was a hell of a position for a white lad to be in, away out there all on his own, suddenly imagining himself morally, and perhaps legally, responsible if blood were shed.

Thankfully I broke out into the deep-trodden impress of the mailman's pad and hurried along it towards the mountains.

That was a nightmare flight running, walking, jogging, in black darkness keeping to the pad by foot-touch and sound, arms warding off the brambles and grasses that walled the pad higher even than a man's head. How some of those supple branches swished stingingly back across one's face! What gasping halts as the pad vanished down some broken ravine! – and all the time driven by fear of a green-eyed dog at my heels. This was Assan's pig country, the very track along which he loped to get into the big scrubs. How tirelessly he would be travelling now if his little brown legs we.re loping along the trail behind! It would have been a mad fight in the dark, after I'd shot his dog.

The massed blackness of the Big Scrub was a relief, and a fright, after the grass-hemmed track of the plain. That track here vanished into a sheer black wall which rose to the sky. The mailman's pad, I knew, bore to the left, where it climbed straight up the stepping boulders of Stucke Gap, declared to be the steepest, rockiest climb for horses in the Commonwealth. They had to plunge like mountain goats up those rocky zigzags. The only other path was the rarely used one I now plunged into, through the Twelve Mile Scrub that filled the great valley dividing Mount Romeo from Mount Hartley. Groping hands touched clammy tree-trunks, while feet felt for the slippery roots that were guides to the way. The brush of palm fronds across one's face, the fear of stake and thorns tearing his eyes, the rebound of canes upon his shins telling him he was off the track were torturing. A moaning wind was rolling along the gorge. Sometimes it roared down in gusts from the summit of Mount Hartley far above. Then a branch would snap and fall crashing in the darkness. Fire-flies floated past and vanished. The splash of unseen creeks and the otherwise rarely broken silence gave one an awful feeling of being quite alone in some uninhabited dream world.

But it was better here than on that lonely pad on the plain. A man could breathe here; he could shoot the dog before turning on Assan. In the darkness each man would have his chance.

Just at dawn I was out of the scrub, actually laughing at the silvery light showing among the forest trees. Birds called in sleepy awakening from valley and mountain side, a blue-tinted jackass chuckled to the coming sun. The world seemed just wonderful again. And how welcome was the first sign of man -the winding sluice race of a scrub-edge tin-scratcher. A few miles farther on and I was at the Rossville pub, waking lazy Bill Cleary from his snug bed. Assan could come if he liked now. A native saddled a horse while I gulped a hasty breakfast. Then I set out along the thirty-mile tin-mine's road to Cooktown, arriving there in the afternoon, delighted at the sight of Dick Welch in the old man's yard, greasing packsaddles. Quickly I explained the hurry. Dick laughed in boyish delight, eager for details. He thought the affair a great adventure.

"Why worry?" he smiled. "All the better if someone's killed, it's more exciting. Wish I'd been there. It's not your fault, anyway, you didn't kill anyone. The police can't do anything to you."

Dick's smiling philosophy was jolly comforting, if not altogether convincing.

"I've got the horses paddocked at the Four Mile," he consoled. "The tucker is already in the pack bags in the shed. We can get away if you're still thinking of old Assan!"

"He'll follow me to Cooktown for a certainty, immediately he comes to his senses. But he won't travel any farther north – he doesn't know the country. Get the horses right away, Dick; it would be stiff luck to stop a bullet at the last moment. Has there been any sign of the Filipino?"

"No. He hasn't come into the bay, and you can bet your life he won't."

"Well, get the horses in while I go up to the Signal Station and see if they've sighted the cutter. I'd just like to feel sure that the little coloured girl is safe, and I'd like to camp a few miles out of town to-night, too."

Up on Grassy Hill overlooking the town was the trim white Signal Station, with the caretaker in charge at his ceaseless job of watching for vessels coming from north and south.

From the closed-in glass veranda, with a deep feeling of thankfulness, I watched a tiny cutter beating past towards Cape Bedford, heading towards the distant north. The cutter had taken as long to do her thirty miles by sea as I had to do fifty overland.

"That's that Filipino *bêche-de-mer* fisher," nodded the caretaker as he handed over the telescope, "I wonder what he's doing running north with a woman on board and not calling in? He's beating against a head wind too."

I gazed at Mee-lele through the telescope, bringing her right close to me. She was sitting on the tiny cabin roof, gazing back towards Cooktown. The Filipino was at the tiller; five native seamen lazed up forrard. The wind whipped around in a freshening from the sou'-east; I could see the cutter responding as I gazed. Almost it seemed that the craft had just dawdled along to hasten now in farewell.

Mee-lele was gazing straight at me. Did she instinctively know it? It may have been only a boyish feeling, but I sensed somehow that she was a little lonely, unhappily pensive. I watched the cutter until she merged like a seagull into the evening mists. A queerly unhappy lad handed back the telescope.

Dick and I rode off seeking new adventures. They came, too, and I feel they will not cease even after the Great Adventure here.

Aboriginal Chief. , Queensland, by Charles Kerry.

www.ingramcontent.com/pod-product-compliance
Lightning Source LLC
Chambersburg PA
CBHW030936090426
42737CB00007B/453